Dr. B. L. Renfrow
Springfield, Ill

Mch-1949

CAN
PROTESTANTISM
WIN
AMERICA?

OTHER BOOKS BY THE AUTHOR

CAN
PROTESTANTISM
WIN
AMERICA?

CHARLES CLAYTON MORRISON

HARPER & BROTHERS
PUBLISHERS NEW YORK

I-X

CONTENTS

FOREWORD

THIS BOOK has been written as a tract for the times. It does not pretend to be a permanent contribution to literature or theology or any other subject whose problems are perennial. It faces a specific contemporary situation and undertakes to deal with it in the most candid terms, with the minimum of fastidious concern for style and systematic organization.

The situation which it confronts is the predicament of Protestantism in American life. I believe that Protestants, in general, are not aware of the reality and seriousness of their situation. They too easily cherish an illusion of progress and strength which derives from the parochial habit of measuring Protestantism in terms of local or denominational successes, while disregarding the emergence and trend of powerful forces outside of Protestantism. These forces, I maintain, have been carrying American society away from Protestantism for two or three generations. Not only so, but they have left their mark upon the churches themselves, appreciably weakening their spiritual morale.

Over many years, the predicament of modern Protestantism engaged the author's attention in the editorial columns of the *Christian Century*. But I have long felt that the urgency of the situation called for a more sustained and thorough analysis. As the reader will discover before he has gone far in these pages, I believe that the task which Protestantism confronts in modern America is too great for it as it is now constituted. I have endeavored to show how great the task is, how insufficient for its accomplishment Protestantism is, in its present sectarian form, and how radical and comprehensive a change is required if America is to be won to the Christian faith in the terms in which Protestants conceive it. If I could state it all in a sentence, I would say that this book is a plea for Protestantism to be itself, that is, to be truly, consistently, unitedly, and militantly Protestant.

The title of this book was prompted by the example of my colleague, Harold E. Fey, who had published in the *Christian Century* a notable series of articles entitled, "Can Catholicism Win America?" I followed in the same publication with a number of articles asking the same question concerning Protestantism. My articles have been largely rewritten and supplemented with much new material for the making of this volume.

C. C. M.

September, 1948

CAN
PROTESTANTISM
WIN
AMERICA?

~ I ~

HOW STRONG IS PROTESTANTISM?

THREE MAJOR FORCES are now bidding for ascendancy in the cultural and spiritual life of America. These forces are Protestantism, Roman Catholicism and Secularism. To say that they are bidding for "ascendancy" is not to ascribe any dark or illegitimate purpose to any of them. It is only to say that each is profoundly in earnest in holding and proclaiming its convictions, and that each is incompatible with the other two.

There are some religious faiths among us which do not take themselves so seriously. They frankly admit that they have no desire to win converts. Such faiths provide religious sanctions for particular groups—racial or traditional or cultural. The principle at the center of such faiths does not claim to be a universal but a partial one. They allow to other faiths a parity with their own and, by invoking what I think is a false conception of tolerance, thus reduce all faiths to a common denominator. Unhappily, many Protestants and some Protestant churches have fallen into this error, with the result that their own faith has been diluted to something approaching sentimentalism. But this is only a marginal phenomenon. Protestantism, historically, takes its faith seriously. It regards itself as the carrier of a universal principle of reality and of the

1

ultimate meaning of human existence. The missionary spirit is of its essence.

Protestantism, Catholicism and Secularism are all possessed of the missionary spirit. Each is determined to mold the character of American culture. The legitimacy of such a purpose cannot be questioned. In the forum of tolerance maintained by our democratic system, our cultural democracy is thus exhibited as a living reality. In this forum, divergent or conflicting beliefs may become reconciled. Or the issues which they raise may become obsolete and fade out. But so long as they are tenaciously held and advocated, they stand in a competitive relation with one another.

Of the three forces which I have just named, each is out to win America if it can. Secularism has made great strides in the past century in capturing large areas of the American mind. Of this I shall have more to say in later chapters. Likewise, Roman Catholicism has greatly extended its influence and is integrating its forces and gathering strength for still further gains. What of Protestantism? Is it also gaining? To ask this question after having conceded that both Catholicism and Secularism have made formidable gains in American society would seem to imply that a negative answer is required. Manifestly, these three forces, representing three-sided contradictions, cannot all be gaining at the same time. Certainly the gains of Secularism in America have been chiefly at the expense of Protestantism, though Catholic leaders will freely grant that their church also has suffered from the popular indifferentism to religion which is the fruit of a secularist attitude toward life. And while it is not yet apparent that Catholic gains have taken an appreciable toll of Protestant strength, it is equally true that Protestantism has made no measurable gains at the expense of Catholicism.

In determining the present status of Protestantism, it is necessary to keep in mind the fact that it was clearly and for a long time the ascendant faith of the American people. If Protestantism were a newcomer in American society, it could now count its gains without reference to its two rivals. But Protestantism has been here from the beginning of our national history. Until recent times it had virtually no competitors. Catholicism was represented by a small minority largely localized in two of our states, and practically negligible in its influence upon our public life and our culture. And Secularism as a conscious philosophy was confined to scattered individuals or small groups of theoretical atheists or agnostics whom the general community, no less than the church, regarded as heretics, or at least as peculiar persons.

But now Catholicism has become a formidable system spreading out into all the states and exercising a powerful influence in public and cultural life. Secularism has infiltrated into wide ranges of the common life, where it exists either in outright negation of Christianity or in indifference to it. On its good side, Secularism expresses itself in many positive forms of ethical activity, in social service and welfare work under a humanistic motivation that operates in detachment from both Protestant and Catholic church organizations. This so-called "Christianity outside the church" has, by and large, gained prestige chiefly at the expense of organized Protestantism. Unlike Catholicism, Protestantism has never been able adequately to integrate the humanitarianism of Christianity into its ecclesiastical system. The reason for its failure at this vital point is found, I think, partly, if not chiefly, in its preoccupation with interests and concerns forced upon it by its sectarian divisions. The maintenance of these divisions consumes an undue proportion of the spiritual and humanitarian resources of Protestantism on their own upkeep. This, however, is getting ahead of our story. What concerns us now is whether Protestantism is gaining.

The easy way to measure the strength of Protestantism is to count numbers—the gains or losses of its membership. This method calls for careful scrutiny. Its results may be deceptive. Periodically, the government census reports the statistical position of the religious bodies of the country. The headquarters of the various denominations also gather statistics showing present number of congregations, number of members, number of ministers, value of church properties, and so forth. In general, most of the Protestant denominations show a gain in membership, by decades if not always by years. This gain is checked against the increase in population and usually shows an advance on population by a slight percentage. The inference drawn from these numerical data is that Protestantism is still going strong, and the churches are encouraged in such a belief. This inference, however, calls for examination.

Increase in membership is one factor in determining Protestant strength, and it is an important factor. A church that does not grow by numerical expansion, that does not win converts and thrust its vitality into ever new areas, obviously does not grow at all. The missionary impulse is of the essence of any faith that takes itself seriously. A church that does not grow in numbers over a long period of years should earnestly examine its position with a skeptical eye to discover the cause of its static condition. There are denominations within the orbit of Protestantism which have entirely lost their evangelistic vigor. They are kept alive by family memory, or by pride in a cultural tradition which centers, perhaps, in a theological doctrine that once had a certain vitality but has become obsolete. Sometimes such churches are kept alive by virtue of endowments or other vested interests accumulated in an earlier period, thus affording resources for maintenance which the present membership would be unable or would lack sufficient motive to provide.

But if particular churches that do not grow numerically should critically examine themselves to find out why, it is no less incumbent upon Protestantism as a whole to inquire whether its apparent numerical strength reflects a moral and spiritual strength commensurate with its membership. Without discounting the significance of statistical growth, we would thus have to define other criteria for measuring the strength of Protestantism. Numerical growth is not the only criterion, and if it is applied without reference to other standards of measurement it may lull the churches into a false complacency. Numerical data indicating progress and strength may actually hide other data indicating arrest and weakness.

We have got to ask such questions as these: How seriously do the members of Protestant churches regard their membership? How deep-going are the commitments which the church evokes in the life of its members and in its appeal for new members? How intelligent is the membership with respect to the meaning of the Christian faith? How firm is the bond of loyalty that holds the members together? How conscious are the local church and the denomination of their organic relation to the whole of Protestantism?

Such questions suggest qualitative criteria, in contrast with a merely quantitative standard for measuring Protestant strength. They cannot be answered by counting heads, and they cannot be easily answered at all, for they refer us to imponderable matters which are beyond the reach of any statistical method. Yet they are not beyond the reach of intelligent analysis. It should be possible to make a comparison of present-day Protestantism with that of former times with respect to such imponderables and to decide whether Protestantism is becoming stronger or weaker in its interior life.

But such an inquiry is only the beginning. We would then have to examine the situation in which Protestantism stands in relation to the non-Protestant religious forces and the secular institutions which have risen to great power in American society. We must not commit the fallacy of looking only at Protestantism and measuring its strength or weakness by what we find there. We must look also at the whole cultural, political and economic scene within which Protestantism lives. Our question will then be: Is Protestantism growing in influence and spiritual power faster than these forces and interests external to itself are growing? Here the ratio of Protestant numerical growth in relation to populational growth becomes a secondary, though not a negligible, consideration. Protestantism cannot claim to be winning America merely because it is adding members to its churches if the preponderant interests of American life are being drained off into rival faiths or secularistic concerns.

Thus the problem of measuring the strength of Protestantism is threefold. First, it is quantitative: Is Protestantism growing in numbers? Second, it is qualitative: Is Protestantism growing stronger in its interior life—in spiritual depth, in an intelligent grasp of its faith, in the bonds which make for its solidarity? And third, it is relative: Is Protestantism advancing in relation to the other forces which are competing for ascendancy in American culture, or is it just holding its own, or is it being outdistanced and overshadowed by them?

Mere growth in numbers may induce a false confidence. It does not follow that Protestantism is growing stronger inwardly, that is, qualitatively, because it is growing larger statistically. It is conceivable that its numerical growth may be maintained by processes and appeals which betray inner weakness rather than strength. I believe, as a matter of fact, that this is the case. Nor does it follow that it is growing stronger relatively, that is, over against other forces in our society, because it is growing quantitatively and/or qualitatively. The primary question we are asking is: Can Protestantism win America? To answer that question we must ask: How strong is Protestantism today? And the answer to this question requires that we apply all three criteria—quantitative, qualitative and relative.

The quantitative is the least crucial of the three, though it must be taken into account. No discussion of statistics beyond those already referred to will be required in these chapters. It is the qualitative and the relative strength of Protestantism that will claim our attention. Statistics will not enable us to measure Protestantism in either of these dimensions. We shall be dealing, as I have said, with imponderables which elude the statistical method. What is required is insight, awareness, a mental emancipation from sectarian provincialism and from the illusions of merely local particularities. Our task will be to see American Protestantism as a whole, to measure the quality of its spiritual life by the standard of the Christian faith, and to define its position in contemporary culture in relation to other forces which, like Protestantism, are striving to mold this culture.

Obviously, this will not be a simple task, and whatever conclusions are reached will not have the exactness of the statistical method. There will be room for argument over the facts educed and the conclusions reached. But it is high time that the argument should begin! I may as well state at the outset that the conclusions will not be reassuring. On the other hand, they will not be defeatist. But I have no desire to give a "pep talk" on the splendid progress which Protestantism is making in American life. We have our special denominational cheer leaders whose professional function it is to keep us all feeling optimistic. This is an important function in carrying on the practicalities of church life. But such optimism, generated in order to "put over" specific projects, must not be allowed to hide the realities of the total Protestant situation.

We shall endeavor to look at Protestantism with an eye as dispassionate as our concern for its welfare is profound. We shall take up first the relative position of Protestantism in the cultural scene of American life. This will be followed (Chapters VII-XI) by an analysis and appraisal of the interior condition of Protestantism, disclosing the self-imposed handicaps under which it operates. The final chapters (XII-XVI) will be devoted to the development of the concept and implications of an ecumenical Protestantism.

~ II ~

THE PROTESTANT SITUATION

WE CANNOT take stock of Protestantism in present-day American society without comparing it with its own past. Is Protestantism as strong today as it was, say, two or three generations ago? That it has a much larger membership, and the increased resources which this numerical advance has brought, is not in question. But we have already decided that its strength cannot be adequately measured by this numerical growth alone. Two other criteria must be applied. One of these concerns the interior strength of Protestantism; the other concerns its relative strength in comparison with those forces in American society which are competing with Protestantism for ascendancy in its culture. We shall take these in reverse order. It is the relative criterion which we are now to apply. And to do so it is necessary to see the Protestant situation of today in comparison with its situation in an earlier period.

Let me first say a word about the relevancy of this criterion of relativity. I am proceeding in the conviction that Christianity, in addition to its inalienable concern for the eternal good of human souls, is also concerned with the temporal good of mankind. Its mission cannot be fully stated in terms of the rescue of individual souls from the grip of sin and their

9

entrance upon the life eternal. Christianity holds itself responsible also for the character of civilization. "The kingdoms of this world," it proclaims, "are become the kingdom of our Lord and of his Christ." To bring this potential sovereignty of Christ down to earth is the acknowledged task of both Protestantism and Catholicism, despite their radical and irreconcilable differences.

A strong religious faith that claims universality is bound to affect the culture of its habitat. It infiltrates into the political, the economic, the intellectual, the artistic areas of life and tends to mold the laws and customs of its culture into an ethos marked by its own spirit, its own ethic and its own ideology. In the degree in which it is the outstanding or ascendant religion in a national community, it is the source which supplies the ultimate presuppositions upon which justice and education and manners and all social relationships rest.

Protestantism once held this ascendant position in the American community. The question we are now asking is whether its influence in American culture is as potent as in former times. If the answer is negative, as I believe it must be, our task is then to seek for an explanation. The explanation may lie either in the inner weakening of Protestantism or in the emergence of external forces which are hostile to it or, if not positively hostile, have drained off popular interest in religion into other fields. It may lie, as I think it does, in both. But whatever the explanation, the fact of such decline in cultural influence will mean that Protestantism is not winning America *now*, though this leaves entirely open the question whether it can ultimately do so. The attempt to measure the strength of Protestantism in relation to the forces which stand over against it today is, therefore, to apply not only a legitimate and relevant criterion, but a necessary one, if we are to understand the present Protestant situation.

Before the last third of the nineteenth century, American life was characterized by forms of association marked by relatively elemental simplicity. It would be superfluous to describe the simple life of those "horse-and-buggy days." Its features have been depicted too often to require repetition. Modern youth can visualize them only in imagination, but some of us have memories extending back to the edge of that period. It was then that Protestantism was the ascendant religious faith in America. It had no strong competitor on the religious level, and the temporal interests of society left room enough for thoughtful consideration of the claims of Christianity and for the practice of one's churchly duties.

These duties were reinforced and brightened by the face-to-face sociability which congregational gatherings made possible. There was no organized mass stimulation of entertainment in the community such as we have today, and the church naturally drew people into its orbit by the occasion it afforded for the spontaneous expression of social feeling. Moreover, the church was the chief center of the community's culture. The minister usually outranked his parishioners in general learning, and his sermons brought instruction as well as spiritual edification to his people.

But more important than all else, the mind of the Protestant community itself and, hardly less, of the non-churchgoing part of the community was well furnished with religious knowledge. They knew their Bibles, their hymnals, their creeds, their denominational doctrines and histories, and could give heed to an unconscionably prolonged discourse with an intelligent understanding exceeded only by their patient endurance. They had learned these things not only in the church but in the home, which made a distinct place for religious practices and instruction. In the family circle theological talk, Bible reading, religious literature and family worship furnished the mentality of both youth and adult with what our psychologists would call a religious "apperception mass," thus guaranteeing that public worship and the minister's sermon would have intelligible meaning.

In a word, Protestantism in that period had positive convictions concerning the Christian faith. These were not always such convictions as we today would emphasize—some were trivial and unworthy of the heat which they generated—but they gave intellectual and moral strength to the church. The general community—even the non-churchgoing part of it—accepted the chief premises upon which these convictions rested: belief in God and the acceptance of Christ and the Bible as divinely authoritative. Thus the whole intellectual milieu presented a congenial field for an aggressive propagation of denominational tenets in particular and the Protestant faith in general. Public education was quite unaware of any reason why its pedagogy should exclude the major premises of the Christian faith. The culture of America was predominantly and, in large part, profoundly Christian, and predominantly Protestant.

In these brief references to earlier Protestantism I am not concerned to appraise the doctrines or customs to which I have called attention. Nor do I write in any spirit of nostalgic longing to return to these earlier days. I am aware that these sketchy references have oversimplified the simplicities of the period, and that an adequate account would require many qualifications. The features to which I have called attention have been selected because of their contrast with the conditions within which present-day Protestantism exists.

Great changes have come about in the habits, the mood, the intellectual outlook, the associational contacts, the family life, the moral standards, the general mores and the cultural composition of the American community. The question we are asking is, Has Protestantism kept up with these changes in a degree which justifies the belief that it is making progress in winning America? My reluctant answer is that Protestantism in relation to its contemporary environment is much weaker than it was in relation to its environment before these changes occurred.

The complexity of modern life has displaced the simplicity of former times. Great magnitudes of social organization and communal mores which did not then exist have emerged in modern society. The community's interests which used to gather relatively unimpeded around the Protestant churches have been drained off and dispersed into other forms of social and cultural preoccupation and habit. Protestantism's vital contacts with the general community have been reduced and weakened by these preoccupations. The new social magnitudes are not all overtly hostile to Protestant faith; but where they are not, the general preoccupation with them represents an appreciable falling away of the community's former respect for Protestant Christianity.

This is only another way of saying that Protestantism in the American community has been reduced to a relative position of far less prestige and potency than it enjoyed in the earlier period. These new magnitudes stand over against it as competitors, challenging its ascendancy in American culture. They present Protestantism with a task for which the simple and direct methods appropriate to an age of simple and unorganized individualism are no longer adequate.

Whenever I reflect on this situation, a familiar scene comes to mind. It is that of which Trinity Church in the city of New York is the center. This venerable edifice at the head of Wall Street once commanded the surrounding area. But today it is dwarfed by the vast skyscrapers which surround it. It is the same edifice, but its architectural supremacy is challenged by the many-storied magnitudes which have arisen on all sides.

The analogy must not be pressed beyond its architectural imagery. For all I know, the activities centering in Trinity Church may be as significant and fruitful as in the past. Nor am I suggesting a contrast between these church activities and the financial and commercial activities centered in the sky-scrapers. The analogy is strictly confined to the architectural relation of the church edifice and its surroundings. This, I believe, is a picture of Protestantism in the American com-munity. In the simple cultural scene where it was once ascendant there have arisen great magnitudes of social cus-tom, interest and organization in relation to which the cultural significance and power of Protestantism have been dwarfed. With these we must reckon if we are to understand the present situation of Protestantism.

In these chapters we shall be viewing "America" as some-thing more than a geographical entity or a populational entity. We shall view it as a cultural entity—that is, as a state of mind. Protestantism, to win America, must deal with America as a state of mind. It will, therefore, be our first task to analyze this America, to discover its cultural character if we can, to bring to light the forces which have produced it and are sustaining it—all this for the purpose of defining the task of Protestantism in the actual America which it is out to win to the Christian faith. The effect of such an undertaking will be to dispel some cherished illusions, but this negative result will surely be offset by the sense of reality which such an analysis should yield.

What are these magnitudes which have arisen over against Protestantism? One is, of course, the Roman Catholic Church, a consideration of which will require a special chapter farther on. The other magnitude is secularism. But secularism is a general category and must be examined in terms of the specific factors operating in American society to produce it.

Before examining these factors, it is important to have in mind a clear understanding of what is meant by secularism. The term refers to "this world." Secularism is an outlook on life limited to this world only. It either denies or has no interest in affirming that human life has any meaning beyond the immediate experience of its events. It accepts each event or moment of experience in its immediacy, and lives from day to day, from year to year, in no broader context than that of life's temporal process. Secularism is not concerned to ask or to expect an answer to the question whether human existence has any ultimate meaning. That is, it lives in "this world" only. Christian faith affirms that this world and this life have a meaning which transcends and encompasses each moment and event of immediate experience. Secularism, in so far as it becomes a conscious philosophy, denies this basic Christian affirmation. It is thus the absolute opposite of Christianity. But secularism may also exist without any conscious dogmatic basis or expression. It may represent only unreflective indifference to religious values. It is in either or both of these meanings that we shall use the term "secularism" in these chapters.

In both its dogmatic and its unreflective forms, secularism has been growing with greater rapidity in American culture than Protestantism. There are many factors which explain this growth. I have chosen five which I consider the most obvious ones. They are (1) our secularized system of education, (2) our preoccupation with science, (3) our organized and commercialized entertainment, (4) the emergence of organized labor, and (5) the extension of the function of the state.

To the first three the following three chapters will be devoted. The last two are merely stated without elaboration, but the reader will be able to apply for himself the same general principle upon which the others are analyzed and discussed. These all are new emergents in our culture. They represent vast concentrations of social preoccupation against whose tough grain Protestantism in our time has to make its way. The Christian faith was, in the earlier period, the basic pattern on which the fabric of American culture was woven. This pattern has gradually disappeared or, where it still survives, is only doubtfully basic. Other patterns have taken its place. These represent the major preoccupations of the community's conscious interest. Protestantism has given no convincing evidence that, in its present state, it is able to penetrate these preoccupations and awaken a vital response to the realities of the Christian gospel.

~ III ~

PROTESTANTISM AND THE
PUBLIC SCHOOL

THE SYSTEM of general education in the United States presents to Protestantism one of the most formidable magnitudes which it confronts as it seeks to win America to the Christian faith. It also affords a measure and an explanation of the degree in which Protestantism has lost its former ascendancy in the national culture. Our educational system has been the most powerful influence in determining the mind-set of generation after generation of our youth. With respect to religion, this influence has been exercised under a theory of neutrality which has excluded all instruction in religion from general education. Thus, on a vast scale, the mentality of our citizenship has been "neutralized" on a basis of virtual ignorance of the Christian faith and of religion in general.

However, this neutrality is not merely neutral. It is negative. It takes the form of secularism which, when not overtly hostile to religion, is ignorant of it and indifferent to it. Protestantism has been consistently loyal to the public school system. The fact must now be faced that Protestantism has been losing the mentality of one generation after another of

17

its own youth to a powerfully implemented system of education whose end product will be a national community in which Protestantism has, if any place at all, only a marginal or survival position.

Our American educational system was established over one hundred years ago in the sound belief that a democratic form of government resting upon the consent of the governed could be maintained only if its citizens were intelligent, informed and responsive to high ideals. Universal education, provided by the democratic community itself, was the answer to this fundamental need. Prior to this revolutionary decision, education had been chiefly the function of the churches. Protestants welcomed with relief the shifting of the burden of general education from the church to the secular community or the state. They believed that they could supplement the work of the public school with effective religious instruction in the church and the home.

It has now become clear that this division of function between the public school and the churches has not been a success. The modern home is notoriously incompetent in this field. The Sunday school with its one hour a week of religious instruction, by volunteer teachers, under conditions of slack discipline, is barely more than a gesture toward education. It cannot command the respect of pupils accustomed to the vastly superior methods, discipline and prestige of the public school. The result is that the curve of religious literacy and of respect for religion itself has been steadily downward for more than three-quarters of a century. American society is increasingly a secular-minded society.

This is true of the general community. But it is also true of the churches themselves. Today the membership of the churches is characterized by a profound ignorance of the

Christian lore, and by a deplorable lack of knowledge and of intelligent conviction concerning Christian truth. Attachment to the church is based on superficial sentiment derived in large part from family memory, or on the sociabilities which the church offers, or on the personal popularity of the minister, or on other peripheral attractions which are totally insufficient to provide the church with the spiritual power in the common life commensurate with its numbers and with the social responsibility which its gospel lays upon it. The simple fact is that the churches of modern Protestantism are running on the momentum of their fathers' faith—or their grandfathers' faith—rather than generating their own power by a vital faith of their own.

Protestantism has been slow in recognizing what a secularized public school system has done to American culture in general and to Protestantism iself. In the conflict between secularism and religion, secularism has been winning all along the line. This is in large part due to the fact that our educational system has been delivering to society and to the churches one generation of youth after another who are almost totally illiterate with respect to the most important subject matter which it should be the business of a well-rounded education to provide.

Protestantism has been greatly weakened in its inner character by this kind of education. The result must not be viewed alone in terms of *children*. For these children have become the adult membership of Protestant churches. The mentality of the entire body of American Protestantism has thus been fashioned under the influence of the secularized public school.

Americans in general, including Protestants, have accepted uncritically a traditional taboo on the inclusion of religion in general education. This taboo arises from an erroneous interpretation of the constitutional principle of separation of church and state. And it is radically inconsistent with the fundamental theory upon which our educational system rests. We shall consider the constitutional aspect presently. Let us now consider wherein the exclusion of religion is inconsistent with modern educational theory.

Modern educators conceive the school as a method or agency for introducing .each new generation into the wisdom and the values which the community cherishes. Its function is to provide the growing child at each stage of his growth with the knowledge that will initiate him into an intelligent participation in the cultural values and the practical responsibilities which make one a true citizen of the community. The teaching profession is the expert to which the community commits this infinitely delicate and important business of orienting its children in the world of nature and humanity into which they have been born.

There are, of course, many other factors besides the school which influence the child's orientation. But the school provides the comprehensive and systematic way by which society opens the doors of its culture and extends its welcome to each new generation. The school thus conceived is a microcosm of the community. Whatever the community holds to be significant in its own life tends strongly to find its way into the pattern in which the teaching profession organizes the curriculum of the school. It is on this principle that the curriculum includes instruction in science, art, economics, politics, history, literature, even business. The curriculum is thus, in theory, a replica in miniature of the common life.

The school sees millions of citizens marching to the polls, and it teaches civics and politics. It sees millions at work in factories and offices, and it teaches economics and business methods. It sees millions entering galleries where sculptures stand and pictures are hung, and it teaches the history and canons of art. It sees throngs crowding great halls where symphonies and operas and plays are rendered, and it teaches music and drama. It sees all the people living in homes, and it teaches domestic economy. It sees innumerable workers in academic laboratories and technological departments of industry, and it teaches science. It sees its society cherishing great traditions, and it teaches history and literature.

For religion, however, the school has a blind spot. It does not see the millions going to the churches. It does not ask why they go, what is in their minds, what they do in church, what literature they read, how their churches are organized, what social concerns engage them, what differences exist among them, out of what history and tradition all this devotion has sprung, what significance this vast phenomenon of religious faith and organization possesses for democracy and culture. To ask such questions and to answer them has been traditionally forbidden by our educational system. The public school does not know that there is such a thing as religion in American society.

Of course, this does not mean that educational leaders and teachers as individuals do not know. They are, as a rule, religious men and women. I am referring to the educational system and the teaching profession, not to the individual teachers. I believe that most educators see that the ban upon religion is contrary to their own theory. Their pedagogical conscience is restive under an interdiction which violates the integrity of their profession.

The inevitable effect of this interdiction is to create a negative prejudice against religion in the mind of each new generation issuing from the public school. The impression is made that religion is not a significant social interest at all, or at most that it is only a marginal one. The puny efforts of the churches to give religious instruction are measured in the mind of youth over against the formidable institution of public education in which religion has no place.

Some two decades ago, the leaders in Protestant religious education, reinforced by many leaders in the general teaching profession, devised a plan known as "released time" to remedy the situation. Under this plan, school authorities were petitioned to allow the churches to enter the public school system with their own teachers and offer religious instruction to pupils segregated according to their parents' creeds. Many local school boards in all parts of the country accepted this offer. A specific hour or half-hour of school time was "released" to the churches for this purpose. In some communities, the classes were held in separate rooms in the school building; in others, in church buildings.

The movement was flourishing in many states without legal opposition. It was assumed that because the released time was available for use by any religious body—Protestant, Roman Catholic, Jewish—there could be no valid objection. Finally, however, a suit was instituted in Champaign, Illinois, challenging the released time practice on constitutional grounds. The case went to the federal Supreme Court which, in March 1948, rendered an 8-to-1 decision that the practice was unconstitutional.

The court's ruling has been variously interpreted. By some it was regarded as a blow at any possible program of teaching religion in the public schools or state-supported colleges and universities. I believe this was an erroneous interpretation. The general question was not before the court. The specific question arising in released time practice was whether the *churches* could constitutionally enter the public school system to teach religion. The court's decision forbade the schools to permit this. It did not forbid the school itself to teach religion. The released time practice was disallowed because it involved a union of church and state which the Constitution prohibits.

It was not merely the use of the school building upon which the court's decision turned. This feature in the Champaign practice was taken into account, but its relevance was marginal. The central question which the court asked was not, Where do the classes meet? but, Under whose jurisdiction are these released time classes while they are receiving church-provided instruction in religion? The facts submitted to the court showed that they were under the jurisdiction of the state, represented by the public school authorities. The taxing power of the state and its compulsory attendance law were made available to the churches to provide religious instruction to public school pupils while they were "in school." The state provided the children and the churches provided the instruction. The institutional functions of state and church were thus woven together. Such an interlocking of the institutional activities of the church with the legal and tax-supported regime of the public school was a use of the civil law and the taxing power of the state for "an establishment of religion." It was a union of church and state at that point, and the court declared such a union unconstitutional.

The question as to the legal right of public schools to give instruction in religion by its own regular teachers has never come before the courts. In all probability a test case would come up if the practice was adopted. But it is hardly conceivable that the Supreme Court would find either in the Constitution or in its own precedents any ground for dictating to the local community what it should or should not include in its public school curriculum.

If, however, the subject matter of religion is included in the curriculum of public schools, two restrictive limitations are clear from the court's decision in the Champaign case. One is that churches may not do the teaching. The other is that the school itself may not teach religion in a manner that tends toward the "establishment of religion," that is, toward a union of the state with any church or churches. There would be no violation of the "establishment of religion" clause of the First Amendment should a public school or state university include religious subject matter as an integral part of its curriculum, provided these limitations were adhered to.

But can the second limitation be adhered to? Can religion be taught on the same pedagogical basis as other subject matters? I affirm that it can. My confidence is based upon the competence of the teaching profession to provide the way. The reason why religion has not been included in the public school system does not lie in the Constitution, but in the community which supports and controls its public schools. The community is divided into many sectarian groups, and the assumption has long prevailed that no way could be found upon which a general consensus of the community could be attained for the inclusion of religion in the curriculum. This assumption has become a taboo. Time was when the assumption was probably true. But the time has now come to challenge it. And the challenge should come from the teaching profession, whose theory of its own vocation is stultified by the arbitrary refusal of the public school to recognize religion as a major social phenomenon and to impart to the youth of each generation a knowledge of its significance in history and in contemporary culture.

In order to see this as a practical possibility, it is necessary critically to come to terms with what is meant by "teaching religion." The problem has been confused by an ambiguity in this concept. It may mean two different things. It may mean (1) the inculcation of religious attitudes and devotions, together with the indoctrination of particular beliefs. In this sense religion is taught in parochial schools and in all Protestant Sunday schools. In this sense also it was taught under released time. Such teaching of religion is generally known by the more thoroughgoing term, "religious education." Teaching religion in this sense is prohibited in the public schools and we should be grateful that it is. The political community of which the school is an instrument must keep its hands off the religious devotion of the people. This is a function of the home and the church—a church independent of the state and voluntarily supported by its members.

Or teaching religion may mean (2) the imparting of knowledge concerning religion. Perhaps this can be more clearly stated from the point of view of the pupil instead of the teacher. "Teaching religion" would then be the *study* of religion. It would be entirely beyond constitutional bounds to prohibit the *study* of religion in the public schools. Mr. Justice Jackson, in his separate but concurring opinion in the Champaign case, wrote a paragraph which deserves to be quoted in full:

While we may and should end such formal and explicit instruction as the Champaign plan and can at all times prohibit teaching of creed and catechism and ceremonial and can forbid forthright proselyting in the schools, I think it remains to be demonstrated whether it is possible, even if desirable, to comply with such demands as plaintiff's completely to isolate and cast out of secular education all that some people may reasonably regard as religious instruction. Perhaps subjects such as mathematics, physics or chemistry are, or can be, completely secularized. But it would not seem practical to teach either practice or appreciation of the arts if we are to forbid exposure of youth to any religious influences. Music without sacred music, architecture minus the cathedral, or painting without the scriptural themes would be eccentric and incomplete, even from a secular point of view. Yet the inspirational appeal of religion in these guises is often stronger than in forthright sermon. Even such a "science" as biology raises the issue between evolution and creation as an explanation of our presence on this planet. Certainly a course in English literature that omitted the Bible and other powerful uses of our mother tongue for religious ends would be pretty barren. And I should suppose it is a proper, if not an indispensable, part of preparation for a worldly life to know the roles that religion and religions have played in the tragic story of mankind. The fact is that, for good or for ill, nearly everything in our culture worth transmitting, everything which gives meaning to life, is saturated with religious influences, derived from paganism, Judaism, Christianity—both Catholic and Protestant—and other faiths accepted by a large part of the world's peoples. One can hardly respect a system of education that would leave the student wholly ignorant of the currents of religious thought that move the world society for a part in which he is being prepared.

Agreeing fully with the court that the Champaign practice "goes beyond permissible limits," Mr. Justice Jackson argued that the court in future cases "must leave some flexibility to meet local conditions, some chance to progress by trial and error." "The task of separating the secular from the religious in education," he said, "is one of magnitude, intricacy and delicacy," and confessed that he did not know where to draw the line that separates "instruction" from "proselyting" and "imparting knowledge" from "evangelism."

Had the eminent jurist challenged the teaching profession

to do what he confessed he was unable to do, his fine statement would have been perfect. The teaching profession is the expert in this business. There can be no doubt that modern pedagogy could develop a subject matter and a technique of instruction that would give religion the same status in public education which is now given to history, politics, economics, literature and art. Some of these subjects, especially economics and politics, and even history, are as controversially "hot" as religion. Yet the schools do not exclude political science because the community is divided into Republicans, Democrats, Communists and the rest. Nor do they exclude economics, because there are free enterprisers and co-operationists and single taxers and socialists in the community. Modern pedagogy possesses a technique by which it is able to teach these subject matters with such objectivity that the partisan issues involved are transcended and the student is left free to form his own convictions. The same can be done with the subject matter of religion.

It would, however, be premature and brash for any community to undertake this project through the teachers now in its public schools. These teachers have not been trained for it. Nor has any systematic effort been made to develop a subject matter. The project will require the same kind of professional training that is now given to the pedagogy of other subjects. And this training can be received only in the colleges where teachers receive their other pedagogical training. The universities and teachers' colleges are now presented with a great opportunity to make an advance in public education by creating departments in the Pedagogy of Religion, designed to develop a graded body of subject matter and to train teachers in a technique for its presentation.

Such a department might find it desirable to include in its

faculty three broadly trained theological specialists—a Protestant, a Catholic and a Jew. These should be selected as individuals, not by ecclesiastical action or appointment. That is, the project should be, from beginning to end, a pedagogical, not an ecclesiastical, project. It would express, primarily, the conscience of the teaching profession, whose theory of education is now distorted by a system which excludes this vast area of the communal culture from general education.

The project would have to begin close to zero. Tentativeness and much experimentation would characterize its labors probably for some years. There would be skepticism among the clergy of all religious bodies, whose knowledge of the flexibility and resourcefulness of the teaching art is virtually nil. This, however, would not perturb or dissuade a university or teachers' college which once set its hand to this task. It is in the interest of the integrity of the teaching profession to take the leadership in abandoning the truncated kind of education which an irrational and thoroughly undemocratic tradition now compels them to offer.

It must be emphasized that such instruction in public schools as is possible under the Constitution cannot be a substitute for the direct inculcation of religious faith and the habits of devotion by the church itself. The imparting of knowledge of religion as a historical and social phenomenon is not to be equated with the more profound religious education which is a function of the church. The respective functions of public school and church must be kept distinct as well as separate. The school may not take over the function of the church. We have every reason to be apprehensive when the state or the political community undertakes to direct the religious devotion of its youth. That way lies totalitarianism.

The church has no grounds to complain of the *irreligion*

of the public school. It is the *religious illiteracy* of the youth-product of the public school that is rightly to be deplored. And it could be equally deplored in·the name of democracy, of general culture, and of educational theory itself, as well as in the name of religion. The churches which deliver their children to the public school for their total systematic education may rightly demand that these children and youth be given sufficient knowledge about religion to create some intelligent respect for it as a social and historical phenomenon and thus enable the churches to proceed with their own task of religious education without having to deal, as now, with a mental vacuum.

Meantime, as the Protestant churches face their task anew, they will do well to recognize and carry forward certain definite gains made by the promotion and practice of the abortive released time device. Three major convictions prompted it, and these must be conserved and built upon. One was the pathetic insufficiency of the Sunday school, considered as religious education. A second was the necessity of weekday time for systematic religious education by the churches. The third was the faith (actually demonstrated in released time practice) that Protestantism would do its part in weekday instruction unitedly.

1. The Sunday school now calls for a radical reorientation. Though it cannot satisfy the requirements of religious education, it cannot be dispensed with. Its function will always be unique in any system of dealing with the church's children and youth. This is so if for no other reason than its close juxtaposition with the church's worship service on Sunday. It is possible that the element of worship should be given a much larger place in the Sunday school and the element of instruction a subordinate place. This would probably lead to

a closer integration with the regular worship service. In any case, the home must be brought into closer co-operation with the Sunday school. The Protestant home has not been doing its duty by its own children. Church leaders have too easily written it off as a hopeless asset in religious education. To this problem Protestantism must address itself with fresh imagination and prayerful concern.

2. The concept of regular weekday religious instruction by the churches has now been established as a necessity. The same kind of co-operation manifested in the securing of weekday released time can secure from the public school authorities, not merely an hour or a half-hour, but an entire midweek afternoon for a genuine school of religious education. The public school would close for that afternoon. The pupils would not be within its jurisdiction, but under the discipline of their parents and the churches.

The proposal to foreshorten the school week by a half-day would no doubt meet with some initial resistance by the school authorities. It would entail some inconvenience in readjusting the teaching schedule. But there is nothing sacrosanct about the full five-day week. Besides, considerable time is now consumed on numerous subjects and activities of far less importance than the instruction the pupils would receive in a well-ordered system such as the churches would provide on their half-day.

3. Protestant churches in the released time adventure did not divide their pupils along denominational lines, but provided a common subject matter for study under teachers chosen without regard to denomination, in a common classroom or church building. This opens up inspiring possibilities in connection with the half-day a week program just indicated. With the development of this program it would soon

appear in many parish-communities that a building specially constructed for this purpose would greatly facilitate the educational process. Not only so, but it would represent the permanent institutionalization of religious education by the community's united Protestantism.

Thus each community or parish would have a Protestant "parochial school," independent of the public school, but not a competitor of it or a substitute for it. The parochial school building would be so constructed that its appointments would not only be available for, but would suggest, innumerable interdenominational uses to which it could be put in addition to the half-day of religious instruction. The Sunday schools would, appropriately, continue to be held in the churches, especially if the element of instruction, as suggested above, was subordinated to the element of worship.

If Protestantism is to win America it must take up the religious education of its children with the same seriousness which characterized its churches before the public school came into existence. Prior to a hundred years ago the whole of education was the function of the churches, and the Christian religion was a dominant interest in its curriculum. Protestantism too complacently shifted its responsibility to the public school, and fell under the illusion that its mere gesture toward religious education in the Sunday school would be sufficient. It is now all too apparent that this was a tragic mistake. The former sense of church responsibility must now be restored.

Protestantism cannot long maintain its position in American life while it allows its children to grow up in religious illiteracy. Its devotion to the public school gives it the right to demand that the ban on religion in the curriculum be removed. But it must project its own unique and inalienable teaching function in terms far more comprehensive, systematic and purposeful than it has yet conceived. Catholicism with its full-time parochial schools is in a position to take advantage of the vacuum in the general culture created by the secularization of public education. Until Protestantism awakens to the fact that its position is vulnerable to Catholicism on one hand, and to a secularized educational system on the other, its hope of winning America is blindly unrealistic.

~ IV ~

PROTESTANTISM AND SCIENCE

CLOSELY ALLIED with the secularized American educational system is the vast and pervasive enterprise of modern science, which also has arisen to great power since Protestantism was the ascendant faith in American society. The scientific enterprise has become the major preoccupation of the modern mind. Its success has altered the relative position of Protestantism in America. If Protestantism is to win America from secularism, it must win science.

I say it must win science, not win America away from science. Science is solidly entrenched in its position. Its marvelous development, however, has carried a large bloc of our cultural mentality away from Protestant Christianity. The scientific way of thinking, the scientific ideal and the scientific method of gaining and validating knowledge have made Christian faith difficult and, in many areas, have crowded it out altogether. Where there was once good reason to expect a response to the claims of Christianity, Protestantism has for a long time been talking into a deaf ear.

Science has rendered a service of inestimable value to the Christian faith. It has compelled theology to think with new imagery of God's relation to both nature and history, and to

33

reinterpret many of its traditional concepts in the light of the kind of universe that is envisaged by scientific cosmology.

The earlier "conflicts" between science and religion were not crucial. But between them a new tension later arose more radical and serious in character. Science came to think of itself, not as a helper and corrector of faith, but as a challenger and competitor. Through the social sciences, it entered the field of human behavior where it confronted religion directly. The claim was made by many scientists, though not by all of them, that religion must now give way, that science is the true messiah for which the world had long waited, and that man's salvation will be found in the enlightenment which scientific knowledge of human behavior will put into his possession. Into wide areas of popular thinking this view has infiltrated. The situation thus concerns Protestantism in its practical approach to American culture. Plainly, Protestantism has not been winning *this* America, but American mentality has been steadily drifting into scientific secularism.

The time is especially opportune just now for science and faith to sit down together in mutual respect and critically examine what each is doing, what each is not doing, and what neither should presume to do. For Protestantism to make it its business to open up such an avenue of intercommunication between them would result, I believe, in their becoming partners, rather than competitors for a monopolistic position in modern culture.

The atom bomb, with all its implications, has shed a new light upon the whole scientific enterprise. The messianic claims formerly advanced by many scientists have been radically shaken in both the professional and the popular mind. Grave questions are now being asked concerning the role of scientific knowledge in man's history. Is it good for man to

know so much about nature and her secret processes? Has
man the moral strength to maintain his human dignity while
possessed of such power as modern science gives him? Such
questions inevitably recall the Greek myth of Prometheus who
stole fire from heaven and gave it to man, thus starting
primitive man on his long pilgrimage in the way of science
and the arts. But the gods were wroth with Prometheus, not
only because they were jealous that man should be possessed
of knowledge that belonged to the gods alone, but because
they feared that finite man was incapable of possessing such
knowledge without using it to destroy himself. And they
punished Prometheus horribly for his treachery.

The astounding achievement of science in its final penetration of the ultimate secret of cosmic energy has brought
mankind to the point where it will be determined whether
Prometheus was right or the gods who tortured him were
right, whether scientific knowledge will prove to be a blessing
or a curse to humanity. Scientists contemplate their consum-
mative achievement with solemn foreboding. Their attitude
is the most significant aspect of the present situation. Scientists
had always looked forward with confidence and pride to the
successful conclusion of every project which engaged them.
But now, the ripened fruit of centuries of scientific labor
emerges in a form of knowledge which threatens mankind
with suicide! Like the parents of an unborn child whose birth
has been awaited with hope and joy, but which, when the
child is delivered, proves to be hideously deformed, science
now shrinks from its own offspring.

The scientific fraternity, reflecting on the terrifying possibilities of the new knowledge they have made available to
man, can hardly refrain from reviewing the whole history of
their vocation in the light which their present achievement

throws upon it. Though all their achievements hitherto have been announced as benefits and blessings for mankind (as indeed they were, and as indeed this final penetration into the secret of cosmic energy might be), there was always a hidden ambiguity in them.

In what does this ambiguity consist? It consists in the inability of science to say whether its knowledge is good or bad for man. It may be either good or bad for him. It depends upon the kind of man he is. And the kind of man he is depends upon something other than his possession of scientific knowledge. That is, science is not the messiah whose mission it is to bring salvation to the world. Its own masters and devotees have now divested it of the messianic robes with which some of their predecessors clothed it.

What is the burden of the exhortation which our scientists, like flaming evangelists, now address to their fellow men? They proclaim, in effect, that science has now reached the point in its development where it becomes supremely imperative to do something about man. And they prophesy doomsday unless their warning is heeded. They do not state their message in precisely these words. Their thinking has not yet got down to that depth. But that is what their appeal really is. What they say is that it is dangerous beyond imagination to allow the atomic bomb, or the knowledge by which to construct it, to lie around loose where man can get at it. It must be put under control. And this must be some form of universal control. But the very concept of universal control implies that something must be done about man. This will be apparent if we examine the proposals which the scientific fraternity is now vigorously advocating.

There are three major concepts under which our scientists propose to make the world safe against the imminent possibility of its destruction by scientific knowledge. One is world government. Another is world community. The third is universal education. To achieve any one of these objectives is obviously to do something about man. The question we must raise concerning each of them and all of them together is whether they can do enough about man to make the world safe both for man and for science.

It is proposed that the safety of civilization demands a world government under which certain functions exercised by the present anarchic sovereignties of our independent nations shall be pooled in the single sovereignty of a world state. The atom bomb and the scientific knowledge for its production and all other military weapons, together with the power to make war and prepare for war, must be surrendered by the individual states to a world state which shall be clothed with power to keep the peace.

But a world state presupposes the existence of a world community. Without such a world community, a world government could not be sustained, even if it could be set up. Manifestly then, the problem of world security in the atomic age is to develop a world community that will make a world government possible. How shall this be done? The scientists and educators stress world-wide and intensive education as the means of creating world community. No doubt, education is an indispensable factor in the creation of world community. But the value of its contribution will depend upon the kind of education that is offered. Most of our scientists and educators are thinking in terms of the kind of education we have in the United States and Western civilization generally—a system dominated by scientific method and thoroughly secularized by its complete exclusion or virtual disregard of religion. This kind of education will not generate world community.

It has not done so in the United States. On the contrary, here it tends to undermine the spiritual basis of our communal unity by sapping the vigor of those cohesive forces represented by historical tradition and vital religious faith. Our educational system, as we saw in the previous chapter, has fragmentized and atomized our American culture. Our unity increasingly finds its chief expression at the superficial level of a common loyalty to the nation-state, a unity which attains its maximum when the nation is at war, and seems to require continual peacetime preparation for war in order to maintain itself. This loyalty, artificially nourished and even exploited by the state, tends toward stark nationalism. But nationalism is the prime enemy of world community. An educational process which delivers to society one generation after another profoundly lacking in critical inhibitions against nationalism is unworthy to be exported to other lands as a means of generating world community.

The primary trouble with the world is not its lack of knowledge, whether knowledge be conceived as scientific knowledge or philosophic wisdom. The world lies in chaos because it lacks devotion to the living God who alone can create a world community. No solution of the predicament of man in the atomic age seems possible except one which is found at the deep level of religious faith. But having said this, we must not imagine that we have said much. We have only identified the level at which any solution of the problem may be found. The task of creating a world community does not consist in getting all mankind to be religious. Man is already religious enough! He is incurably religious. One might almost say that he is automatically religious. St. Paul told the Athenians that they were "extremely religious," yet he went right on preaching to them the Christian gospel. Religion, as such, is not necessarily good. There is bad religion as well as good religion, demonic religion as well as divine religion. The primary thing that is the matter with the world is this: It is devoted to bad religions. Its religiousness is oriented toward false gods.

Nationalism is man's latest religion. It has taken the forms of fascism, nazism, state Shintoism, sovietism. Each of these is a religion, fitted out with a cultus, a body of dogma and a supreme object of devotion—the nationalist state. There has grown up in America a religion of humanism which, largely under the influence of science, denies the Christian God, and sets up a god of its own whose name is Man.

Now, Christianity affirms that these all are false religions, demonic religions, because their gods are unworthy of man's worship. Their gods are idols, the work of man's hands or of his darkened imagination. These false religions are the real trouble makers of the world. They deify race or class or an ancient culture or the nation or man himself. There can be no world community while they hold sway. Education will not break their power. They flourish chiefly among peoples who have had education for a long time or are eagerly developing it, and they all pay homage to science as the means by which their religious faith is to be triumphantly established. These many forms of demonic religion are instinctively hostile to Christianity, because, if for no other reason, it is Christianity alone which exposes their true inwardness and so enables us to recognize in them the most formidable enemy of world community.

There are other religions, far older than nationalism or humanism, which we cannot characterize as bad, but as mixtures of good and bad, of the true, the partly true, and the false. These ancient faiths, such as Buddhism, Hinduism,

Taoism, Islam, have many elements in common with Christianity. Christianity is not out to destroy them, but to liberate them, to set them free from the dark mists which cloud their true insights. It approaches them, not in the spirit of hostility with which it approaches the idolatrous religions of nationalism and humanism, but in the spirit of friendship and appreciation, and offers itself as the fulfillment of the partial truths and the struggling aspirations which these religions dimly express.

There are three radical tests which any religion, offering itself as an adequate faith for mankind in the atomic age, must pass. These tests are all open to objective consideration. In the first place, such a religion must possess in its inherent genius the resources for creating world community. Secondly, such a religion must be able to live side by side with science in mutual understanding and respect. Thirdly, it must be able to do something radical about man. I affirm that Christianity alone meets these requirements. No other religious faith is able, by its inherent genius, to create a world community, a universal *modus vivendi*, competent to survive the terrifying hazards of a scientific age.

All the evil religions of nationalism and humanism are obviously disqualified under these criteria. True, they can satisfy the second: an evil religion can live side by side with science in mutual cooperation. But these evil religions cannot create a world community, nor live in one. By their inherent nature, they are disruptive of world community. As for the ancient religions of the East, they are virtually irrelevant to world community. By and large, they are individualistic and self-contained, and quite unaware of any responsibility for the character of civilization. We are left, then, with Christianity as the one hope of the world in the atomic age. Can

Christianity justify and support this hope? Can it meet and satisfy the tests to which a religious faith must submit?

As to the first test—its power to create a world community—I shall have to be content with a single assertion. Christianity is the only religion which has the dynamic of universality, the spiritual resources, the adaptability, and the inherent sense of moral responsibility for the character of civilization which world community requires. I should like to expound and document this assertion, but must devote the remainder of this chapter to a consideration of the second and third tests, namely, the special fitness of Christianity to live side by side with science, and its unique ability to do something about man.

Is Christianity fitted to live side by side with science in a world community? The ready answer is that it has already lived with science for a long time. Together, they became the predominant cultural forces in Western civilization. But this ready answer is countered by the reminder that for the past century and more there has existed a "conflict" between them. Science developed a consciousness of its own self-sufficiency which assumed a quasi-messianic character. It was tempted to seize the oriflamme from the hand of Christian faith and to lead mankind to salvation by way of scientific knowledge.

But now the atomic bomb has brought this conflict to an end. The scientists themselves have settled it by capitulation. When they turned from their climacteric achievement and became evangelists warning mankind against the destruction to come, they acknowledged the non-messianic character of their vocation. They confessed that science cannot save the world but that it may destroy the world, that the hope and possibility of salvation lies elsewhere than with science, that the salvation of the world from science itself is the supreme desideratum of the atomic age.

It remains, now, for scientists to perceive the bottom fact about the state of the world. This fact is not man's ignorance of scientific knowledge. The bottom fact is that the world is infested with bad religions. It worships false gods. The problem of creating a world community is fundamentally the problem of getting rid of these false gods and their religions. The only way to get rid of a bad religion is to cause it to disappear by the introduction of a true and good religion. And the only religion that can drive out the bad religions from a science-minded civilization is one that can do something radical enough about man to make it safe for science to endow him with scientific knowledge. Such a religion, and only such, can live side by side with science in a world community. This, I affirm, Christianity alone can do.

Science and Christian faith now stand together with a common outlook upon the future. With one voice they declare that the future of the world is precarious. Christianity has always been haunted with the conception of the end of the world. And with one voice they declare that the future of the world is precarious because of man. When they talk about man and the nature of man they are standing on ground long pre-empted by Christian faith. Science is now looking at man with new eyes. It sees the same thing in man that Christianity has long clearly perceived. Science has no word for it; but Christianity has. That word is *sin*.

We are thus brought to the third test to which any religion which offers itself as an adequate faith for the atomic age must submit: it must be able to do something radical about man. Of all the religions and philosophies which the mind of man has embraced throughout history, none has penetrated to the depths of man's nature as has Christianity. It alone has explored the innermost region of man's being. It finds there the sources of human goodness—in conscience, in love, in high aspirations. But it also finds conflict, an inner war between "the flesh and the spirit," because of which the native goodness of man never attains an unmixed realization. The consciousness of this frustration Christianity calls *sin*. Though it applies the word also to the overt act, which it calls sinful, yet the word carries a profounder reference.

In the unique way in which Christianity conceives "sin" it applies to the very constitution of human nature out of which the sinful act comes. Sin, it says, is an inherent and inescapable condition of inner conflict or tension which belongs to the nature of man as man. It is the conflict between man's freedom and his finiteness. He is free, but he is also finite. His freedom is always limited. In the exercise of his freedom, he easily forgets that he is finite and so runs afoul of the moral order by deeds of self-assertion which frustrate conscience and love and high aspiration, causing injury to his fellows and bringing injury and often destruction upon himself. In his freedom he can create or he can destroy. He can create if he remembers that he is finite; he will surely destroy if he forgets that he is finite and remembers only that he is free.

Christianity now asks the scientists to look steadily and profoundly at that in man which makes it dangerous for him to possess such knowledge as science has given him. It is sin that makes scientific knowledge dangerous for man—the sin of forgetting his finiteness in the exercise of his freedom. The more knowledge he has, the more precariously he lives, and the more dangerous he is to himself. For knowledge is power, and the natural man loves power, perhaps above all things. With the increase of power man is tempted to inflate his freedom and to discount his finiteness. Science has vastly widened and deepened man's knowledge and thus vastly increased his power. But, as science, it has nothing at all to offer for the restraint or discipline of man's exercise of this power. This is the reason why scientists now turn aside from their vocation and appeal to their fellow men who are not scientists to deliver mankind from the immeasurable danger with which scientific knowledge imperils man's very existence.

Now, Christianity makes it its business to deal with man, not alone on the surface level of his conduct, but at the radical source from which his conduct springs, namely, the precariousness of his inner nature due to the imbalance between his finiteness and his freedom. It introduces a super-human control over man's exercise of his freedom so that he can live safely with scientific knowledge and so that science can live safely with him. The primary task which Christianity sets for itself is to keep man reminded of his finiteness! And to keep him so reminded of it that the consciousness of his freedom is not impaired, but enhanced. How does Christianity proceed to do this?

It proceeds by confronting man with his Creator!

When God comes, the half-gods go—the false gods, the idols man has made—the evil gods and their religions go when man is confronted with the living God to whom he owes his very existence. Face to face with his Creator, man becomes aware of his creatureliness, of his finiteness, of his presumption in the egocentric exercise of his freedom. In one inclusive word, he becomes aware of his sin—the sin that makes him pretend to be better and stronger than he really is, that prompts him to clothe his self-righteousness with virtue, the sin that flatters his ego with fine excuses for his misbehavior. Standing before his Creator man cannot do otherwise than confess his creatureliness. Like Job, when God appears, he says: "I had heard of Thee by the hearing of the ear; but now mine eye seeth Thee. Wherefore, I repent in sackcloth and ashes." Or like Isaiah in the temple, when he saw the vision of the holy God, he falls upon his face and cries, "I am a man of unclean lips!" Or like the publican beating his breast, he prays: "God be merciful to me, a sinner."

Bending thus in contrition and humility before his Creator, something happens to man. It is a miracle of grace. He hears a voice saying, "Rise, stand upon thy feet, and I will speak unto thee." Follows then an unworded and ineffable conversation between finite man and his Creator. Who has ever been able to report that colloquy? But Christianity proclaims that it knows One who overheard it. That one is Jesus Christ. He has told us what God says. He told it from a cross! What was there made known became the Christian gospel. It is the good news of the Creator's forgiving love. This "forgiveness" means far more than the cancellation of man's guilt for his overt misdeeds. It means that the Creator himself takes man's sinful nature into his own healing care, that he actually shares man's sin and expiates it in his own suffering love. And not in this initial moment only, but always, so long as man walks humbly with God in unremitting awareness of the inner peril to which his finite freedom continually exposes him.

From this initial launching of a new life, with a new heart, man's freedom passes into a new dimension. No longer irresponsible self-assertion, his freedom now becomes self-surrender to the will of God who has given Himself so fully to him. Only in such surrender to his Creator is man safe with his freedom. Only when his finite freedom is made captive to the will of

God is he truly free. Only then is he safe with the knowledge which science gives him.

But we have not stated the whole case for the Christian faith when we have exhibited its power to change the natural heart of the individual man. For Christianity is also out to change the nature of man's communal life. Christianity holds itself responsible for the character of civilization, no less than for the character of the individual person. It holds that a world community competent to sustain a political world order can come into existence only by a regeneration of communal man, answering, on a public and universal scale, to that regeneration which it is able to accomplish in the private experience of the individual. That is to say, a world community is possible only if mankind, through the cultural organs which express its corporate existence, is kept constantly confronted with its Creator, the living God, whose acknowledged presence drives out and destroys all the false gods which are disruptive of world community

Science surely has a stake in a religious faith that is able to do this thing with the nature of man. For science, too, needs to be saved. It needs to be saved from utter futility. To what good end is all this knowledge that science has unloaded on the unready spirit of man if he remains unworthy to be trusted with it? Every enlightened scientist in every laboratory the world over must now be reviewing the whole history of the scientific enterprise and asking himself, Is all this labor, this devotion, to be in vain? Is all the future labor of scientists to be performed under the imminent threat that man will turn its fruits to his own destruction? Only a profound and transforming religious faith can save both man and science from such a fate. And the Christian religion is the only faith that comes to grips with man in those depths of his nature out of which are the issues of life. This is the meaning and the poignant relevancy of the Christian faith for the atomic age.

Science and Protestant Christianity now come face to face, but in a different mood from that which would have marked such a meeting before the atom bomb fell. Each has been chastened—science by disillusionment, Protestantism by its dereliction. Before Hiroshima, science was at the zenith of its ascendancy in modern culture. In its race with Christian faith it was winning, decisively. Western civilization had been permeated, not only with scientific knowledge, but with the belief that science was the true savior of mankind. Science had become, in effect, a religion. It had undercut and was dissolving the concepts by which the Christian faith made itself articulate. These concepts had been for centuries the conscious or unconscious presuppositions from which Western culture had derived its standards of art, of literature, of education and of conduct. The conceptual structure of our culture which once had been Christian was being displaced by the conceptual structure of science.

Protestantism itself stood in awe of science. Its apologetic for Christianity took on the tone of an apology. Or, in desperation, it retreated into an obscurantist and irrelevant fundamentalism. Western civilization, largely under the influence of science, had gone pagan. Science did not care and Protestantism did not perceive what had come to pass within three generations. The worship of the living God, the Creator of man, the Builder and Upholder of civilization and the only Power able to bring to realization a world community—the worship of this God had become hardly more than a respectable formality in Christendom itself. The real gods of this pagan secularism were those fashioned by man's paganized imagination.

Cannot both Protestantism and science be brought to repentance? Science, for its blindness and its egoistic delusion that it was the bringer of salvation; and Protestantism, for its sycophancy in burning incense at the altar of science? We should cherish no illusions. Science is here to stay, and its knowledge will grow from more to more. Knowledge of the Promethean fire still burns in man's veins. The perils of such knowledge will not stop man's pursuit of it. The world into which we are now being ushered will, *if it survives,* be penetrated more thoroughly than ever with scientific knowledge. We shall have unimaginably better modes of communication, swifter modes of transportation, easier modes of production, more terrible modes of destruction. In every area of human living, science will so revolutionize man's social habits that men of the future will look back at our time as we now look back at the "horse and buggy days." In that science-minded world community, everything may be changed—everything except man. Scientific knowledge will not change the nature of man.

Cannot the scientific mentality of our time, both professional and popular, be made to see the stake it has in a religious faith which alone can save science from the fear of man and the whole scientific enterprise from futility? If Protestantism is to win America, it must, I repeat, win science. But it can do so only if it grasps firmly the substance of its essential gospel and proclaims it with the conviction which its everlasting truth deserves.

~ V ~

PROTESTANTISM AND COMMER-
CIALIZED ENTERTAINMENT

IN SEEKING an answer to the question, "Can Protestantism
win America?" we are viewing America not merely as a
geographical entity, nor merely as a populational entity, but as
a cultural entity, that is, as a state of mind. The contemporary
mentality of America is not as responsive to the Protestant faith
as was that of an earlier period of our national culture. It has
been drawn away from religion into secularism. In these
chapters, we are in the midst of an analysis of this secular
mentality, seeking for the factors that have produced it. We
have found that our secularized educational system and the
widespread acceptance of the messianic pretensions of science
have been generating a secular mentality faster than Protestantism has succeeded in Christianizing it.

We have now to consider a third bloc of our cultural
mentality; namely, that formed by the institution of commercialized entertainment. Increasingly, our generation has
delivered its leisure into the keeping of organized purveyors
of entertainment, whose enterprises cover the entire nation,
whose motive is financial profit, and whose offerings are
designed to reach and hold the attention of the mass mind.
To accomplish this, the predominant appeal is made to the

senses. Habitual exposure to these forms of entertainment leads to an overstimulation of the senses at the expense of reflective thought. By thus undermining the reflective intelligence of the community, our culture is removed farther out of reach of the appeal of Protestant Christianity.

Before the emergence of this system of mass exploitation of the people's leisure, young and old alike invented their own entertainment. The hours of toil were longer, the margin of leisure for relaxation was narrower, and the facilities for utilizing leisure had to be found by individual or group initiative. But the tempo of living, with respect to both work and leisure, was slow enough to allow reflective thought to maintain itself in a wholesome balance with the sense stimuli received from nature and the simple organization of human society. In such an environment Protestantism could count upon a response to the presentation of its faith. There was time and mental capacity for reflection on the deeper issues of life. A certain amount of idealism and reverence before the mystery of things could be presupposed in the approach of religion to such a mentality.

The development of modern technology has changed all this with respect to both labor and leisure. It has mechanized labor, and increased the margin of leisure. The mass exploitation of leisure by the use of the new techniques in providing commercialized entertainment has become a positive factor in the secularizing of our culture. If we compare the present access of Protestantism to contemporary mentality with its access to the mentality of the earlier period, it can hardly be claimed that Protestantism *has been* winning America during the past two or three generations.

I shall not discuss the *moral* effects of the kind of entertainment provided by the moving picture, the radio, the pulp magazines, the drama, the jazz, the comic strip, the newspaper's exploitation of crime and its endless elaboration of the most intimate and sordid marital revelations in the divorce courts. The moral effects of all this are obvious enough. But there is a deeper question than the moral question. It is concerned with the effect upon the mind itself, upon its capacity to think, to think seriously about life, and to respond to moral ideals and the ultimate values which are the substance of religious faith. Protestantism, I maintain, today confronts a cultural mentality whose capacity to respond to the truth of the Christian faith has been appreciably impaired and shrunk by habitual exposure to the intensive barrage of sensuous stimuli which beat upon the mind almost from the cradle and all the way to the grave.

This has brought about an imbalance between the sensational content and the ideational activity of the modern mind. Ideas can only with great difficulty take root and come to fruition amid the lush jungle of sense stimuli which preoccupy the mental field. The opportunity and the desire to reflect on the profounder issues of life have been crowded out by the very multiplicity of invitations to mental relaxation which are pressed upon the individual by the producers of commercialized entertainment. Their aggressiveness, motivated by huge profits, is too strong for the defenses which ordinary human nature is able to raise against it. These invitations come thick and fast, leaving no adequate interspaces for the exercise of conscious critical reflection. Yielding to their fascination, the appetite for artificial sensation grows by what it feeds on, and what the late Professor Babbitt used to call the "inner check" is reduced to virtual impotence.

This incessant bombardment of the mind with sensuous stimuli has subtly, but profoundly, changed the quality of the mentality of our generation. In producing an imbalance between sensation and reflection, it has inhibited ideational spontaneity by surfeiting the mind with more sensation than it is able to digest. Our prevailing mentality, in this respect, is the exact reverse of the Puritan mentality of the pioneer period. In the Puritan culture the imbalance was overweighted on the other side of the scales—the reflective or ideational side. The sensuous was regarded as intrinsically bad, and was accordingly held under repression by a stern theological intellectualism and moralism. Indulgence of the natural impulses in the gaieties of life therefore lacked the spontaneity and freedom of a clear conscience. This type of culture actually impoverished reflection by shutting out the natural sense stimuli which are required to feed the mind and keep it wholesome.

The human mind is tougher than the Puritan moralists imagined. It can stand, without serious injury, more exposure to sense stimuli than their ethical system allowed for. But when its exposure to the glamorous, the fantastic, the false, the artificial and the merely silly or merely clever becomes habitual, the effect upon the mind is bound to be disintegrative. The aggressive monopolists of the people's leisure, whose profits depend upon gaining and holding popular interest, have succeeded in creating a mass appetite for artificial sensation which spells intellectual decadence. Not only do ideas have difficulty in sprouting in such a mental soil, but ideals cannot bite into consciousness with vigor; they hover over consciousness and evoke a certain moral longing, but this longing tends to expend itself in mere vague sentimentality.

Ours is a sensation-saturated generation. Its capacity to think and to think seriously has been shrunk by the commitment of its leisure to the commercialized purveyors of entertainment. Walter Lippmann, quoting Aristophanes, declares that "whirl is king." We are distraught, and have no cure for our distraction save to seek other distractions. We no longer invent our own forms of entertainment. Why should we when a twist of the radio knob, or a movie palace around the corner, or the endless strips of fantastic nonsense in the "comic" supplement, or the synthetic mystery story, or the public dance pavilion, or the "bookie" in the rear of the neighborhood barbershop, or the restaurant and the "tavern" with their stage shows, provide us with all the "kick" which our jaded senses require without any planning or invention on our part?

This commercialized, ready-to-wear entertainment tends downward toward vulgarity and profanity. The vulgarity is obvious. The profanity is hardly less obvious. It moves steadily toward obscenity, tearing aside the thin veil of privacy that rightly protects the more intimate precincts of life from the cheapening which accompanies their exposure to public display. The purveyors of mass entertainment are put to it to invent new plots and scenes for a public that has already "seen everything." Goaded by this necessity, they inch their way into the sacred areas of morality and religion in search of fresh stimuli for their public. Here, two opposite motifs are utilized. One is intended to shock the moral and religious sensibilities with subtle and sophisticated "digs" at the established conventions which express and sustain morality and religion. A public whose taste has been perverted to the point of seeking after shocks for the sheer thrill of being shocked, actually takes this sort of profanation with gusto.

The other motif proceeds by an opposite tactic. Instead of shocking by smart impudence, it caters to religion by patronizing and exploiting it. The public gets a pleasant thrill by seeing a religious play in such a glamorous setting. But the plots of the so-called religious plays are so patently synthetic and meretricious that their net effect is to profane their subject. The treatment of the church, the clergy (except the Catholic clergy), and the profound realities of religion is distorted and cheapened by the glamor of the context in which such plays are set. Whatever virtue a play of this kind may have is usually washed out by the wild west, the crime, the bedroom or the nonsense play that precedes and follows it.

I am not indulging in any Puritan view of the drama. But a dramatic presentation of religion requires a sincerity and simplicity of which our commercialized entertainment system seems to be incapable. The effect of such theatrical religious sentimentalism upon the mentality of the community is bad. It is part and parcel of the whole irresponsible system whose owners justify its sensational character on the ground that they are "giving the public what it wants." And what the public wants is simply more of what this system has, in great measure, corrupted the public mind to want.

Our commercialized entertainment system is producing a mentality of escape from the deeper and more ultimate issues of life. It blights mental spontaneity—the capacity to react critically and intelligently upon the subject matter which the system offers as entertainment. By undermining standards, it has broken down inhibitions. By breaking down inhibitions, it has corrupted taste. And by corrupting taste, it has stultified judgment. Thus the mind is left relatively inert, possessing its passive function of receiving sensations, but incapacitated to select, reject or evaluate them. The active, ideational function is frustrated because it is swamped by an inundation of sense stimuli so great in volume that the mind is unable to deal with it.

However, the active function of the mind has not been altogether suppressed; it has been deflected. Its power to react critically to subject matter has been transferred to an abnormal interest in technique. The *way* the thing is done and the originality displayed in the doing engage critical attention in compensation for the mind's inability to form a judgment on the thing done. That is to say, subject matter is subordinated to technique. This, of course, is a complete inversion of aesthetic values and moral standards. It also represents cultural decadence. A good subject matter presented with sincerity and simplicity, but with an amateur technique, will be more highly appraised by a healthy-minded society than a bad subject matter presented with technical brilliance and originality. Increasingly, our society has become incapable of reacting in this way.

In an era dazzled and obsessed with the amazing technological development made possible by science, it is not strange that technique has become the idol of education, of the arts and of entertainment, while subject matter has been thrust into a secondary, if not a negligible, place. The genius of science inheres in its technique, its method, its apparatus. These represent its legitimate business. But the case is otherwise with education and the arts. These have taken over the exclusive scientific point of view which, legitimate as it is in science, becomes illegitimate and a sign of cultural decline when it dominates other cultural fields. The decadence of our culture can be understood if we recognize this subordination of subject matter to technique in painting, music and the other arts, including the art of entertainment.

Our ultra-modern painters and composers, lacking depth of insight and inspiration, that is, lacking any profound artistic or musical ideas, devote their talent and skill to the development and display of the technical possibilities of their art. Their productions assail our senses with subject matters so distorted, ugly and dissonant as to cause actual pain to the uninitiated.

The initiated, however, react with a certain delight to these technical originalities. Their enthusiasm is regarded by many as an affectation. But it is not so. They see or hear something the uninitiated do not discern. Preoccupied with technique themselves, they observe or listen in relative disregard of the subject matter and find their pleasure in the demonstration of hitherto unused possibilities of line and color or of the logical development even of dissonances within a consistent tonal framework. Their pleasurable reaction is more intellectual, more "scientific," than aesthetic. It is akin to the reaction of a clinic of medical students to the "beauty" of a successful surgical operation, even though the patient died.

It may well be that, when art again has something true and great to utter, this development on the level of technique will prove to have value. But the obsession of modern art with the "how" rather than the "what" betrays not only its own bankruptcy, but the bankruptcy of our age itself with respect to meaningful aesthetic ideas or subject matter.

We find the same inversion of technique and subject matter in our commercialized entertainment. Few of us realize how drenched our minds are with the flood of nonsense and silliness and grotesquerie and artificiality and vulgarity and profanity with which astonishingly clever technicians intrigue our attention in newspaper, billboard, radio, moving picture, and the smart-set magazines. We have become conditioned to like the smart thing, the quick retort, the wisecrack, the cryptic *double entendre,* and to disregard the subject matter in which this cleverness is purveyed to us. But the substance, too, leaves its deposit in the mind and tends to stifle whatever serious and honest thoughts we may have in our more natural reaction upon the world of reality.

This tolerant fascination with technique in disregard of subject matter is illustrated by the startling change of attitude toward drunkenness. The role of the "drunk" is now portrayed with an artistic cleverness which excites neither repugnance nor pity, but only moronic laughter. The sordid realism of drunkenness as it must be endured by the family of that reeling man (or woman) who passed your window last night, holloing bawdy inanities as he made his heavy way toward home, has given place on stage and screen and air to an artistic idealization as false as the father of lies can make it.

Modern education, too, is the victim of this cultural imbalance between technique and subject matter. Some of our educators are beginning to see that their system has been producing smart people, equipped with certain special skills and possessing that kind of mental alertness which exhibits itself in quick reactions to immediate stimuli, but whose minds are sadly unfurnished with the content or subject matter of our cultural heritage into which a sound education should induct them. The technique of the scientific laboratory has become the idol of modern education. In becoming a science, pedagogy has ceased to conceive itself as an inspirer of wisdom. Its fascination with technique and method leads it to treat subject matter as merely so much "material" upon which to exercise its technical skill. The attainment of this technical understanding of the subject is supposed to constitute a knowledge of it. The values of beauty or wisdom which inhere in the subject tend to be dissolved in this process and leave only dim marks upon the student's mind.

This may be illustrated by the modern method of teaching Shakespeare. In times not so long ago, the aim of professors of English literature was to reveal the depths and heights of human feeling and insight which inhere in his plays, and to kindle in the student an intelligent reaction to these values. The greater passages were memorized, and thus the student's mind was furnished with lofty subject matter for lifelong reflection. Modern pedagogy holds this procedure in frank disesteem. It not only shifts the student's attention to the mechanics of the poetry, but focuses upon the fact that these plays were plays. This leads to a study of the Elizabethan theater, and this to a study of the relation of Shakespeare to the theater of his time. The technique of the drama, as such, thus tends to subordinate the inherent values of the literature, as such.

But it is from the literature, not the drama, that Shakespeare's immortality derives. True, this literature was written for the theater, and its study in that connection has a proper place in education, but such study is not a proper substitute for the apprehension and appreciation of the values inherent in the literature itself. By this process the values tend to be obscured or drained off, leaving a considerably desiccated body of literature whose significance lies outside its own subject matter.

The inversion of technique and subject matter in art, in education and in entertainment has been producing a mentality shockingly uninterested in the serious realities of life. Add to these factors the widespread influence of science in whose field the priority of technique legitimately belongs, and you have a mentality not only uninterested in, but singularly incapacitated to think on, the ultimate questions which find their answers only in the realm of religion.

This general state of mind presents to Protestantism a cultural magnitude which it can hope to penetrate only by dealing with it in its totality, that is, by creating respect for Protestant power at the centers from which this profit-motivated system originates. With respect to art, we shall have to wait, I suppose, upon the wind which "bloweth where it listeth." Unquestionably, an order of genius will some day emerge, burdened by the tragedy and emptiness of contemporary life, to voice the deeper meanings which our mechanized mentality has forgotten how to make articulate.

With respect to commercialized entertainment, Protestantism now finds itself in a weaker position than Catholicism. The latter has already proved its strength in toning down certain flagrant indecencies which were particularly repugnant to its own moral code. But its traditional indifference toward a people's mores in general should inhibit any expectation of support from Catholicism in those other matters in which the Protestant conscience is equally sensitive. The task of saving America from the enervating influence of the commercial exploitation of the people's leisure, rests uniquely upon the shoulders of Protestantism. It must assume this responsibility if it is to save itself and win America.

~ VI ~

ROMAN CATHOLICISM AND
PROTESTANTISM

SIDE BY SIDE with Protestantism in facing America's culture stands Roman Catholicism. Each is a historical expression of Christianity, though wide divergences in doctrine, practice and institution separate them into virtually two distinct religions. Both cherish the hope of winning America, each to its own faith.

Catholicism is proceeding on a bold and highly intelligent strategy. It is now developing and putting forward preachers who address the American public with winsome and persuasive arguments in exposition of Catholic doctrine and tradition. Their preaching is warmly evangelistic. It is directed to the saving of lost souls who wander in the aimless emptiness of secularism. This is a relatively new feature in American Catholicism. The church has not been noted in this country for its preachers. It has been content to produce priests and administrators. Its evangelistic program has been exceedingly cautious. But now it feels no need of caution.

During the past two decades the Roman Church has become consciously secure in its position in American society. It no longer fears that a program of open and overt evangelism might result in waking the sleeping dogs of intolerance.

It has seen the A.P.A. and the Ku Klux Klan condemned and destroyed by enlightened Protestantism, backed by enlightened public opinion in general. It sees Protestantism becoming less and less militant, and wasting its energies in sectarian competition. And it sees the cultural drift away from Protestantism, and within Protestantism, into secularism. It is aware, as Protestantism is not aware, of the emptiness at the heart of American culture. From these considerations, Catholicism now derives confidence to abandon the caution which previously restricted its religious work to activities largely within its own fold.

The Roman Church now feels at home in America. Its reputation as a "foreign" religion has been lived down. Since the days of unlimited immigration, its second and third generations of native-born Catholics have given it a consciousness of being indigenous, and thus of having rights which it was previously slow to press. It now feels free to be itself, to take advantage of every method and expedient, to strike out boldly with all its resources and win America to its faith. The development of a few preachers who have the "feel" of American psychology, who can be trusted with a wide latitude to interpret Catholic doctrine and morals, is a conspicuous feature of its program. Not many preachers are needed, now that the radio is available. One voice can reach the whole American public.

The Catholic radio preacher addresses himself directly to the vacancy, the meaninglessness, at the center of contemporary life and offers salvation to all lost souls who commit their lives to "Mother Church." In this approach Catholicism has, initially, a psychological advantage over Protestantism, because it offers to fill the vacuum with only the barest minimum of responsible reflection and decision on the part of the individual.

Its offer of salvation is a substitute for individual reflection and decision. It asks only for an uncritical acceptance of the church whose hierarchy is the divinely authorized custodian of the truth.

Protestantism, on the other hand, is essentially and historically a religion of the laity. It awakens and releases in the individual soul the sense of its own direct and immediate responsibility to God. It presupposes a personal decision on the *merits* of the gospel. This personal decision is something which a secularized mentality, once it is awakened by life itself to the emptiness of life, is only too willing to evade. It is thus more susceptible to the easier offer of a ready-to-wear salvation than to the acceptance of the responsibility involved in making a personal decision.

Catholicism is thus likely to find a ready response in two types of secular mentality—the sophisticate among the intelligentsia, and the unreflective person representing the great mass whose capacity to think upon the ultimate meaning of life has been shrunk by an absorbing preoccupation with secular interests. In both types, there is a void where wisdom, reverence and faith normally have their source. But life has a way of breaking into this void and awakening a sense of its hollowness and a longing for salvation from the meaninglessness of a purely secular existence. This may occur when the spirit is broken by frustration or tragic grief, or by a haunted conscience, or by any crisis of experience.

When this happens to the sophisticate or the unreflective person, each is peculiarly susceptible to the kind of salvation offered by Catholicism. The sophisticate, because he is a tired intellectual. He wants to be done with thinking. His thinking has brought him no good; it has ended in a blind alley. His will also is tired; he wants to evade the responsibility of personal decision. He is therefore ready to respond to the promise of inner peace and rest by casting his burden upon "Mother Church" whose hierarchy will do all his thinking and deciding for him.

The other type of mind, unaccustomed to reflection upon the deeper realities of life, but awakened now by some crisis experience to ask the questions which only religion answers, is utterly bewildered. Such a mind turns with equal responsiveness to the appeal of Catholicism or Protestantism or any of the innumerable cults or sects—whichever one gets to him first. But Catholicism has the initial advantage here also, for it meets this type of mentality on its own sensuous level with impressive symbolism and the formidable claim of authority.

Thus the secularized mind of contemporary America provides an open and promising field for Roman Catholic evangelism. The opportunity is enhanced by the fact that the Roman Church, despite its great age, seems like a new faith to the American non-Roman mind, which is almost totally unacquainted with the history and nature of Catholicism. This attraction of novelty in the realm of the spirit, which always characterizes a decadent culture, gives Catholicism an appeal upon which it cannot count in a society where it has been long established and widely understood. But in America, the disillusioned or the newly awakened secular mind tends to look upon familiar Protestantism with the prejudice previously formed, while Catholicism seems to come as something fresh and new.

How far this Catholic evangelism has penetrated into American society is not known. It is doubtful that many converts have been made as yet from Protestantism or from the periphery of Protestantism. The publicity given to the conversion of certain highly sophisticated persons should not be taken as a symptom of any large response. But neither should its significance be minimized. The procedure is just getting under way and, in the present state of American mentality, such a procedure, operating without a vigorous Protestant alternative, is bound to produce substantial results in the long run.

It is safe to say that those reared outside of the Roman Catholic tradition who accept the church's offer of salvation, do so without an adequate consideration of other aspects and features of Catholicism. Their yearning for peace and rest and absolution is all-absorbing. Distressed in spirit or conscience, they are naturally in no mood to examine the wider implications of their act in committing their souls to the authority of the Roman Church. Were these implications brought sharply to attention, they would certainly offer strong, if not always effective, inhibitions.

Roman Catholicism can be understood only when it is *seen whole*. It is something else than a way of salvation. Seen whole, it presents itself as a system of irresponsible and authoritarian power—a kind of power which no human institution should presume to possess and exercise, a power which is radically incompatible with both Christianity and democracy, and which carries within itself the seeds of its own corruption. The Roman Church is a monarchical and feudal institution. Its power is embodied in and exercised by a self-enclosed professional class, the hierarchy. This ruling class is entirely removed from any form of responsibility to the lay community of the church. Over it the community has no control. On the contrary, it controls the community. It is the perfect embodiment of the principle of fascism. The hierarchy, with the pope at its head, is the counterpart (or should I say, the prototype?) of the fascist or nazist or communist "party" with the dictator at its head.

This church operates on a principle exactly opposite to that embodied in our democracy and in Protestantism. There are no elections, no referendums, no disciplinary measures in which the lay community participates. Such functions, which are designed by democracy to curb power, to replenish and purify it by a constant flow of the living stream of consent, are unknown in Catholicism. The hierarchy is self-perpetuating, self-contained, autonomous and sacrosanct. Its decisions and deliverances flow from the top down, and claim the authority of Christ himself whose "vicegerent on earth" is its head.

Plainly, the unimpeded extension of the power of the Roman Church in American society will profoundly transform our culture and institutions. The methods by which this church operates to extend its power flow consistently from its nature as a system of irresponsible power. It maintains an amphibian existence as both a church and a state. Naturally, therefore, it detests the American doctrine of the complete separation of church and state, and the collateral doctrine of the political toleration of all religious faiths. In every country where its power is clearly dominant, it asserts its political as well as spiritual supremacy over the state and over the rights of minority religions. In American society it claims all the rights guaranteed by our government to minority faiths, rights inspired largely by Protestantism, but Catholic spokesmen in their franker moments admit that, if or when its present position in relation to Protestantism is reversed, it will operate here also in accordance with its own genius. That is to say, the democratic process radically modified.

But Catholicism has been operating here for a long time in ways that foreshadow its policy in the day of its ascendancy. For more than a century it has been a potent factor in the American political scene. Instinctively, it has searched out the sources of social and political power and capitalized on its access to them. It operates with a degree of solidarity unknown in Protestantism. Its integration with municipal political machines has spread to virtually every large city in the land. Its policy has been to infiltrate the faithful into public office and so gain, if not direct control, a privileged relation to political power. This relationship yields substantial benefits to the church in innumerable favors, direct and indirect, as well as in popular prestige.

Parallel with its exploitation of municipal politics the church entered the public school system of the middle sized and larger cities of the country by way of getting Catholic teachers placed in the schools and Catholic personnel in the school boards. In this it has been aided by its liaison with the dominant political machine. Its interest in the public schools presents an anomaly. The Catholic educational policy is hostile to the public schools. It withdraws its own children from them as fast as it can provide means for the maintenance of its own parochial schools. Why it should concern itself with the operation of these "Godless" schools which it has no intention of supporting and no hope of reforming, is difficult to explain except on the basis of its instinctive urge for power, plus the patronage which this power provides for the placement of the faithful in school positions.

The political activity of Catholicism has, moreover, in recent years, become potent on higher levels than the local scene. The church has gained increasing recognition as a political bloc on the state and national levels. The earlier popular prejudice against voting for a Catholic candidate for public office has considerably subsided, though it may still exist with respect to the presidency. The "religious issue" is rarely raised. Indeed, in many places the shoe is on the other foot—the issue is raised, albeit discreetly, by the Catholic-controlled machine which quietly serves notice that only a Catholic can win.

With respect to many appointive offices, the hierarchy has established the assumption that an office made vacant by death or retirement of a Catholic incumbent must be filled with another Catholic or balanced by a Catholic appointment to an equivalent position. This assumption prevails especially in the judiciary system. It was illustrated recently at the highest level upon the death of Mr. Justice Butler, of the Supreme Court, when it was frankly assumed by the administration that, inasmuch as he had been a Catholic, his successor must, of course, be a Catholic. Such recognition of the legitimacy of a dynastic succession representative of religious or racial blocs in high appointive offices where character and competency alone should be determinative, establishes a vicious precedent in the democratic process.

The political activity of Catholicism on state and national levels has been persistent and indefatigable in its effort to secure public money for the support of parochial schools. The church hierarchy is determined that the burden of supporting its schools shall be shifted from the church to the public treasury. Its long-range policy is to demand that its proportionate share of school taxes shall be diverted to the church for the church to spend as it will. To this end, significant beginnings have been made. In some states the hierarchy has secured the enactment of legislation granting the right of Catholic children to be carried to parochial schools in buses provided by public funds to carry children to public schools. The Supreme Court recently sustained the constitutionality of this legislation. In certain states which provide free textbooks for public school pupils Catholic textbooks are being furnished by tax money for the pupils of Catholic schools.

From such initial achievements, it is only a step or two to the appropriation of public funds in aid of needy Catholic pupils in Catholic schools, for salaries of teachers in such schools, and even for the construction of parochial school buildings. The bill introduced in Congress for the appropriation of several hundred million dollars of federal money to supplement education in the less affluent states has been held up chiefly by the vigorous Catholic lobby which demands that the proposed federal grant shall apply to private, including Catholic, schools as well as to public schools. Thus with buses and textbooks as a beginning, a principle and a precedent have been established which logically lead to the "establishment of religion" by law. There can be no doubt that the hierarchy will press its advantage to the limit.

The most daring political activity of the hierarchy reached a dramatic achievement in 1939. After years of manipulation and pressure, it succeeded in gaining recognition of the Vatican by Mr. Roosevelt's appointment of a "personal ambassador" to the holy see. This was a clear violation of constitutional procedure in such matters and of the democratic principle embodied in the constitutional provision for the separation of church and state. The thin deception under which Mr. Roosevelt, characteristically, sought to disguise the real nature of his action by coupling with it an invitation to the Protestant president of the Federal Council of Churches to come up and see him sometime, was nothing less than an insult to Protestantism.

After the death of Mr. Roosevelt, it was hoped that this illegal relationship would quietly be allowed to lapse. But the Vatican and the American hierarchy had other thoughts. President Truman, in a recent action, so casually taken that he deemed it unnecessary to offer an explanation, reappointed Mr. Roosevelt's "personal" ambassador, this time as "the President's" ambassador.

The issue, thus aggravated, came alive once more. Protestant churches throughout the country again voiced their protest in strong resolutions. A delegation of their official leaders, sponsored by the Federal Council of Churches and including its president and general secretary, waited on President Truman to acquaint him with the disquiet and resentment which the continuance of this official liaison of our government with a particular church had aroused. The delegation received from Mr. Truman positive assurance that the ambassadorship to the holy see would be discontinued when the war is formally ended by the signing of the peace treaties, if not before.

The President's good faith in making this promise cannot be called in question. But Protestants and American citizens in general who sense the implications of this violation of the principle of separation of church and state cannot afford to rest upon this assurance. It can be taken for granted that the hierarchy, both in the United States and at Rome, will bring all its resources to bear to prevent the fulfillment of the President's promise. It can be made politically embarrassing for Mr. Truman to discontinue the embassy. Only the strongest counterpressure by those who see what is involved will assure the promised presidential action. The issue involves the whole question of religious liberty, of the equality of all churches before the law, of the separation of church and state, of the denial of special privilege to any church, and of the constitutional provision requiring confirmation by the Senate of all ambassadorial appointments. It involves, too, in the long run, the question whether the Catholic hierarchy shall be thus given a special access to the supreme centers of power in the American government to manipulate them in the interest of winning America to the Catholic faith.

The Roman hierarchy has come to a position in American

society where it can now exercise its power decisively upon the agencies of mass entertainment, information and opinion. In dealing with the press, the radio and the moving picture, it has in view a single purpose, namely, to create *respect* for the Catholic Church. The industries which operate these agencies have been made vividly aware that it is commercially prudent not to admit anything to their pages or pictures or broadcasts which touches Catholic sensibilities. The exercise of this power has thoroughly cowed these industries. So well established is the code of silence on news prejudicial to the Roman Church that, in the rare case in which it is broken, the hierarchy boldly calls down reprisals upon the violator. This was illustrated when a San Francisco newspaper, two years ago, reported the arrest and fine of a priest who, with a woman companion, pleaded guilty to drunken driving. The result of this breach was the threat of an organized boycott of the offending newspaper, led by the archbishop himself.

Obviously, the exercise of this power of news repression pays positive dividends also. Made conscious of the organized power of the hierarchy with respect to the code of silence, the press and the movies naturally cater to it in other ways. Catholic interests and activities are given disproportionate, if not preferential, consideration. Any reader of the secular press, especially in the larger cities, can sense the fact that Catholic activities and events are treated with greater respect than Protestant activities and events. This not alone in the amount of space and in typographical display, but in the orientation of the news story or editorial itself.

The hierarchy has succeeded in creating a psychology of respect, not to say awe, in the offices of American journalism, which is in sharp contrast with their casual attitude toward Protestant affairs. In this mood the press naturally tends to exaggerate the intrinsic significance and the actual news value of Catholic affairs. It accepts as its own the appraisal which is put upon an event by the official publicity bureau of the church. In dealing with Protestant affairs, the reporter makes his own appraisal, which is usually perfunctory and often pathetically ignorant.

The recent orgy of synthetic publicity in connection with the elevation of certain American prelates to the cardinalate illustrates this positive dividend which the psychology of awe at the hierarchy's power has created in our secular journalism. This event justly deserved radio, newspaper and film attention. But the exaggerated, detailed and long drawn out publicity was so transparently inflated that the source inspiring it and the motive in reacting to the inspiration could not be concealed.

It is not necessary to assume that the hierarchy applied pressure to secure this exaggerated recognition. Its success in applying the negative pressure to establish the code of silence has created a state of mind which automatically appraises such an event out of proportion to its real significance. The effect upon the public mind is as if such publicity said straight out: "This is the real thing; this is the significant expression of the nation's religion; this is the genuine church."

There is little profit in reproaching these agencies for their partiality. The fact is more pertinent than any plea or argument that can be brought against it. And the fact is that the Catholic hierarchy has convinced the organs which influence and reflect the public mind that Catholic affairs have greater public significance than Protestant affairs. This journalistic judgment may, after all, be true. If so, Protestant eyes should be opened wide to its implications. Instead of centering their criticism exclusively on the press, the radio and the films for their servile relation with the hierarchy, Protestants would do well to recognize in this subserviency a yardstick by which to measure the magnitude which Catholic power has become in American society—and, correspondingly, the decline of the public significance of Protestantism. It is a waste of energy merely to grouch about the situation. Wiser would it be for Protestant thinking to turn inward and subject Protestantism itself to a searching examination to discover why its former pre-eminent position in public respect is being superseded by Catholicism.

The growth of Catholic power is manifested in its intelligent approach to two large populational blocs—organized labor and the Negroes. In his series of articles, "Can Catholicism Win America?" Harold E. Fey brought forward much valuable information on Catholic activity in both these groups. The Catholic Church is far ahead of Protestantism in establishing working relations with labor organizations. It has created a labor organization of its own inside the unions, composed exclusively of Catholic members of the unions. It is called the Association of Catholic Trades Unionists—Actu, for short.

Membership in Actu is limited to devoted Catholics. The endorsement of a priest or of two members is necessary for admission. "The Actu does not permit non-Catholics to join, because its fundamental purpose is to spread the teachings of the Catholic Church," says an official publication of the organization. By this wise course the church retains its hold upon its own members, gains a respect among the mass of workers which Protestantism does not command, and at the same time maintains a missionary agency whose fruits in converts to the Catholic Church must be considerable.

The duty of winning the Negro to the Catholic faith has been repeatedly pressed by the Vatican upon the American hierarchy. The latter was cautious in responding in an open official manner until it had sufficiently consolidated the church's position in white America to be able to risk the racial prejudice which a large influx of color into the church might arouse. This hesitation is now a thing of the past. Certain influential sections of the Catholic press advocate an aggressive policy. Missionary and educational operations are already well developed by religious orders. The Catholic Negro membership is now about 300,000. Negro priests are being trained and already some have been ordained. Championship of certain political interests of Negroes has won favor for the church among them. The church has plans well formed which it believes will present to the Negro "an intelligent religion of the kind he will not find in his roaring, ranting Protestant meeting-houses."

A singularly effective device for gaining adherents to Catholicism is represented by its policy in relation to mixed marriages. It is strange that the implications of this policy have not been more carefully examined. Mixed marriages are rightly deplored by the Catholic Church, as they are also by Protestantism. But Catholicism has an extraordinarily shrewd way of turning them to its own account in return for the blessing of the church. It demands that the non-Catholic partner shall sign a pledge promising not to try to change the Catholic partner's religion and to rear any children born of such a marriage in the faith of the Roman Catholic Church.

This is one of the many points at which the church's exercise of its authoritarian principle is violative of the democratic process. True, it violates no statutory law, so far as I know. But there is much more to democracy than is expressed in law. Democracy is a penetrating principle, extending into the most intimate relations of life. In the home, this principle requires that no barriers be raised between husband and wife and no legalistic restraints imposed beyond those which they mutually undertake in their marriage vows. Here the most unrestrained interaction in the realm of ideals and on the deep level of religious faith is essential to the fulfillment of the spiritual concept of marriage. Obviously, the Catholic procedure in mixed marriages inhibits this spiritual freedom. It exploits love itself in its most susceptible moment for the advantage of the church, and subjects the non-Catholic partner to an indignity to which he or she would certainly never submit in any other situation.

In addition to the automatic gaining of the new generation as adherents of the church, the effect of this authoritarian policy in mixed marriages is a clear advantage to the church financially. In thousands of cases, large fortunes formerly in non-Catholic hands have, through this process, fallen automatically into the orbit of the Catholic Church. Every sizable community knows of local instances where this has occurred. A single outstanding instance is that of the Henry Ford fortune. I do not charge that this result enters into the motivation of the practice, but an institution as worldly-wise as the Roman Church would hardly overlook the fact that the financial by-product which it yields is large in present reality and enormous in future possibilities.

Roman Catholicism can be understood only when it is seen whole. Those who listen to the radio preacher hear the better part of Catholicism—the essential Christian gospel which cannot be altogether hid by the elements in its transmission which falsify it. Similarly, the periodic utterances of the pope frequently express the Christian faith in noble words. But Roman Catholicism is something more than these utterances of preacher or pope convey.

Modern Protestantism does not always state its critique of

Catholicism in sufficiently comprehensive or sufficiently radical terms. It focuses upon specific practices such as Mariolatry, adoration of the saints, the confessional and priestly absolution, transubstantiation, holy water and incense, a foreign tongue in worship, celibacy, miracles, relics, isolation of nuns and monks in monasteries, splendor of costly vestments, resplendent parade of the eucharistic celebrations, the claim from Scripture that Christ founded his church upon St. Peter and many other features of Catholicism which are repellent to a Protestant conception of Christianity. These all merit the repugnance of the Protestant mind. But Catholicism has its own way of rationalizing them and making them plausible to the tired sophisticate or the unreflective mind seeking peace and rest in the hour of the soul's distress. Superstition runs through them all, and superstition is the vital principle of Catholicism.

But to focus attention upon such specific features as these is futile so long as the institution as a totality goes unchallenged. The inner practices of the Roman Church cannot be reformed by an outside attack. And they will never be reformed from within. The holders of this vast power will never voluntarily give it up. The inner features of Catholicism will last as long as the institution lasts, for they are essential to its existence. They all reflect its power, a power which cannot be maintained on any other basis, because it is an irresponsible power, resting upon the abject submission of its people, whose submission it is able to exploit for the maintenance of its power over them and the gaining of yet more power in the political and cultural life of the secular community. We do not see Roman Catholicism truly until we see it as a system of irresponsible power, exercised through a self-enclosed sacrosanct ruling class marvelously knitted together in a descending scale of hierarchical authority from the papacy down to the lowest order of the priesthood. The pope claims to receive his power from Jesus Christ, whose vicegerent on earth he infallibly and unchallengeably decrees himself to be. From the sublime sanctions with which its power is clothed the church derives not only the right but a sense of obligation to seek yet more power on the assumption that it thereby brings more honor to Christ.

To see Catholicism in this way is to see it whole. And when it is seen whole it presents itself as something more than a perversion of the Christian faith in its inculcation and cultivation of superstitions. The principle upon which this church is founded is the antithesis of the democratic principle upon which our national community maintains its existence. The divine right of the papacy is the apotheosis of the principle of the divine right of kings, a principle which democracy had to overthrow as it slowly emerged in the modern world and found its consummate expression in the American Constitution.

The Roman Church is thus an exotic and alien ingredient in the social and political life of America. Except in this institution, the democratic principle pervades our whole social order. Not only our governmental activities, but every form of communal organization, from the public school and the Protestant churches to the Rotary club, is democratically maintained. These all operate on the principle of the responsible consent of their constituencies, democratically evoked and registered. Except in the Roman Church, a dictatorship is unknown in our entire social structure. If certain labor unions seem to be moving in the direction of a dictatorship, they are doing so by flouting the theory on which they are set up, and the apprehension which they arouse in the public mind arises from the fact that this development of irresponsible power may lead to the overthrow of democracy in the government itself.

But Catholicism exists in America as an already perfected dictatorship, exercising a power which is not amenable to any form of democratic control. Its incompatibility with both the forms and the spirit of democracy is an obvious threat to the character of our institutions.

The existence and spread of Roman Catholicism thus presents a political and social, as well as a religious, issue in our democratic society. The issue has been only dimly perceived in its political aspect because the American people have little historical background for an understanding of the nature of this church. Besides, the church has only within recent years found sufficient assurance to be itself and to adopt an aggressive program of overt action in furthering its interests. But in countries where Catholicism has had the right of way, its methods are well understood. They are reflected in the political phenomenon known as clericalism. "Clericalism," says John A. Mackay, "is the pursuit of political power by a religious hierarchy, carried on by secular methods and for purposes of social domination." It represents the determination on the part of an ecclesiastical system of power to use the state as an instrument of its will. Clericalism is becoming more and more manifest in America despite the counterbalancing presence of Protestantism and the as yet unshaken tradition of democracy. The ascendancy of Roman Catholicism in America would radically transform our culture and change the character of our democratic institutions.

INTERIM SUMMARY

THUS FAR, we have been looking at the America which Protestantism is out to win to the Christian faith. We have not yet looked at Protestantism itself. Our analysis has disclosed the fact that contemporary American society is strikingly unlike the America of three or four generations ago. This change is profoundly relevant to any religion which aspires to win America to its faith. Contemporary culture, we have seen, has taken on the form of a congeries of blocs or orders or magnitudes of secular mentality. Their being secular does not, of course, condemn them. But their absorbing preoccupation with secular interests presents Protestantism with an entirely different problem from that which it faced in the earlier period of more independent, atomistic individualism.

Of course, the mind of the individual is never really independent of its environment. It is always and everywhere fashioned by interaction with it. But the pressures from environment have never been so massive, so highly concentrated, so well organized and so powerful as are those which constitute the environment of the modern individual in America. These pressures originate in a few large, organized systems which operate for the mass production of a secular mentality as systematically as a Ford factory operates for the mass production of a standardized type of automobile.

We have brought into bold relief three major agencies which

operate to produce this mass preoccupation with the secular. These we have found to be (1) secularized education, (2) the scientific enterprise and (3) commercialized entertainment. Two more, however, of equal importance, were mentioned in Chapter II. One is (4) the emergence of organized labor. This phenomenal development has drawn the great mass of industrial workers into a powerful solidarity whose purpose is to secure justice and the rights denied them under an economic system with which they had previously dealt merely as individuals. The class-consciousness generated by this development presents a massive bloc of mentality which Protestantism, traditionally limited by a bourgeois outlook, and lacking any corporate embodiment of its own strength, finds it difficult to penetrate. The other is (5) the extension of the function of the state, whose paternalism tends strongly to change the psychology of individual self-reliance into a psychology of reliance upon the collective community. The moral virtues stressed by Protestantism have been traditionally individualistic, and it has not yet found in the Christian faith an ethic profoundly relevant to this new collective mentality.

Here, then, are five massive blocs of secular consciousness which have emerged in American culture since Protestantism was its ascendant faith. It is not my contention that they are consciously hostile to Protestantism, or that they exploit a conscious secularist philosophy. My only point is that they represent a complex system of secular preoccupation which, in comparison with the simpler psychology of the earlier period, has pushed Protestantism psychologically out of focus in the contemporary scene. Relative to its present cultural environment, Protestantism has, therefore, distinctly receded from the position it formerly held in American life.

Add, now, to these five secular magnitudes the emergence

of Roman Catholicism which, as we have seen, has attained the status of a formidable competitor of Protestantism for religious ascendancy, and the picture I wish to draw is roughly complete. If these magnitudes, including Protestantism, are all visualized together, aided perhaps by the architectural imagery of Trinity Church and its surrounding skyscrapers in New York city, which I suggested in the second chapter, the reader will have what I believe is a true and objective picture of the relative position of Protestantism in the American scene.

~ VII ~

THE PROTESTANT TASK

WHAT DOES PROTESTANTISM look like when it is seen in relation to the vast and dynamic magnitudes of secular interest and the regimented power system of the Roman Catholic Church? To an outsider, it looks like Trinity Church in its architectural setting. It looks like a survival of an era that is past. It is so regarded by politicians, educators, labor leaders, journalists, and the financial tycoons who control the agencies of mass entertainment. For the most part, they go on their way quite unconscious of its existence. Many of them may be members of Protestant churches, but in their vocational relationships it hardly occurs to them that Protestantism is a formidable entity whose significance is important or especially relevant in their secular world. They have ample reason to be respectfully conscious of Catholicism. But the difference between a Catholic membership of 23,000,000 and a Protestant membership of 43,000,000 does not impress them. The reason is that Protestantism is not corporately oriented toward these great psychological blocs in a manner that commands attention and respect.

Protestantism has not learned to live in the modern world. It has carried over from the era of individualism its structures of organization and its simple procedures that seemed appropriate and adequate then, but are so no longer. Everything around it has changed—the whole structure and psychology of society—but Protestantism proceeds as if it were still living in the middle eighties. It has not grasped the fact that it now confronts powerful collective units of mentality, not merely separate individual mentalities, and that these collective mentalities have been molded by secular interests which religion cannot hope to penetrate by a simple approach to individuals.

Catholicism, on its part, is instinctively and intelligently aware of this collectivist structure of American mentality, and it acts accordingly. It makes itself felt at the centers where mass psychology is generated. Its purpose at these centers, as we have seen, is first to create *mass respect* for the Roman Catholic Church, and then to work through these power centers for building up the church by the acquisition of individuals. It never forgets the individual. Catholicism is political-minded, economic-minded, publicity-minded, education-minded, class-minded, union-labor-minded, race-minded, but the individual is always at the front of its mind. He is the end product which its approach to the collectivity has in view.

But Catholicism does not depend exclusively, as Protestantism does, on an evangelism addressed merely to the individual. Rather, it seems to wait for the individual to come on his own prompting. But its strategy is to make sure that his collective conditioning is such that, when his heart is turned toward religion, the way will be clear for him to turn naturally toward the Catholic Church. Its radio preaching and all its evangelistic efforts are designed to gather the ripened fruit of this collective conditioning.

Protestantism cannot win America until it rids itself of the illusion that American mentality is still individualistic, and that its churches are really gaining because they are recruiting individuals into their membership. The American mind is now predominantly collectivist in its structure. It is molded by a relatively few massive blocs of secular interest, each more or less autonomous, and each under the control of its own center of power. Protestantism, on the other hand, is sectarianized, localized and individualized. It has neither organization nor technique for gaining entrance into, or commanding the respect of, these collectivities.

Protestantism's contacts with government, the labor union, industrial management, the agencies of mass publicity and entertainment, the educational system, the scientific enterprise, even the family, are tenuous, unimpressive and hardly more than wordy. These contacts do not evoke the respect which a strong Protestantism could command. The Protestant churches still depend for the winning of America upon an evangelism that deals with the individual quite apart from his collective context. And when it gains him for the church his allegiance is only half-hearted—the other half of his heart is in the mentality of the secular collectivity to which his church is a stranger.

The above analysis of the contrasting strategies of Catholicism and Protestantism omits certain cushioning qualifications which a perfectly balanced statement would include. But if I were to include them the essentials of the contrasting strategies would be obscured. Protestantism must be brought to see how inadequate is its conception of its task, how insufficient is its strategy and how illusory is its complacent belief that it is winning or, without a radical reorientation of its forces, is able to win the America which it confronts today.

The result of our analysis so far has been to dispel any illusion that Protestantism *has been* winning America during the past three generations or so. But *can* it win America? To answer this question we must now turn our attention inwardly upon Protestantism itself. Here we shall be guided in reaching our judgments by what I have called (see Chapter I) the *qualitative* criterion. Does Protestantism possess the qualities of character, of spiritual and material resources, of organization and of will to win America to the Christian faith?

At the outset, we must get rid of the notion that Protestantism ever did *win* America. By and large, it *was* America from the beginning. Protestants peopled this country and set the pattern of its institutions. The foundations of the union were laid by Protestants and Protestant-minded statesmen. Except Maryland and Louisiana, all the states of the union were settled by Protestants. The early migrations which opened up the west were predominantly Protestant. The ascendancy of Protestantism was not achieved; it was inherent from the start. This historical fact is important. The loss which Protestantism has sustained in the drift toward secularism is therefore not to be measured against any "gain" which it made in the earlier period. The naked truth is that American society was once predominantly Protestant and is so no longer. Secularism and Roman Catholicism now challenge its ascendancy.

It is important to recognize that American secularism is largely apostate Protestantism. This suggests that the primary task of Protestantism is to orient itself, both in consciousness and in organization, toward the cultural mentality which it has lost or is in process of losing. To do so is not only to follow the line of least resistance and of greater immediate promise, but it is, strategically, the only course that will save America from Catholicism. The alternative course is to join direct issue with Catholicism. This, I believe, would miss the mark completely. It would be much easier for Protestantism to divert its energies to its controversy with the Roman Church. It has an arsenal of argumentative ammunition already at hand, accumulated over the past four hundred years, upon which to draw. But Protestants are self-deceived if they imagine that merely by raising an anti-Catholic clamor they will achieve any worthwhile Protestant results.

For Protestantism to allow its energies to be diverted into this channel would only betray its own weakness. Such a course would be merely a compensatory activity, covering up its failure to tackle its own positive and much more formidable duty, that of winning America to Protestant Christianity. Besides, the kind of mentality which now predominates in America is, as we have seen, peculiarly susceptible to the Catholic appeal; and it is easily conceivable that while Protestantism was engaged in a head-on controversy with Catholicism, it would one day be rudely awakened to the fact that Catholicism had actually won the ascendancy. *The true task of Protestantism is to win the very America which Catholicism is out to win.*

I do not suggest that the controversy with Rome should be considered closed and laid on the shelf. Rome is a cultural competitor of Protestantism wherever the two co-exist in the same society. The differences between them are radical and irreconcilable. The ascendancy of one spells one kind of America. The ascendancy of the other spells another kind. It is inconceivable, for example, that a democratic civilization would have been established here had this country been settled by Roman Catholic pioneers. And it is inconceivable that the Latin American countries would be what they are had Pilgrim and Puritan and Cavalier been destined to establish there the foundations of a new order.

The Protestant controversy with Catholicism cannot therefore be excluded as if it were irrelevant to the contemporary Protestant task. But it should enter in only obliquely. For

Protestantism now has a controversy with American culture itself, the culture in which it was long the ascendant and accepted faith. It is this controversy that must determine its frontal and direct orientation. The aggressive activity of Catholicism should provide Protestantism with a reinforcing incentive to arouse itself, to throw off the illusion that it still holds the predominant position in American society, and to meet the formidable challenge which secularism presents to the Christian faith.

Such a reorientation of its consciousness and its resources would have revolutionary results. It would eliminate those trivial controversies which have divided Protestantism; it would draw its fragmented parts together in a solidarity of purpose, and it would generate an irresistible inner compulsion to achieve its own organic unity.

In a word, *Protestantism must now confront the contemporary scene as if the Christianization of America depended, under God, upon it alone.* Catholicism is not an ally of Protestantism in winning America to the Christian faith. No sentimental tolerance should blind Protestant eyes to this fact. There are numerous opportunities on the political and social levels where the two can work together, but they cannot be yoked together on the religious level. They exist in separate dimensions. They move in opposite directions. They have divergent and incompatible aims. They hold radically different conceptions of the Christian religion. Whatever points of apparent similarity exist between them are vitiated by the irresponsible power system that Catholicism is when it is seen whole. By contrast, Protestantism carries the democratic principle up to the level of religious faith and organization. All its American denominations are democratically constituted and maintained—with varying forms of structure running all the way from the mass-meeting type of democracy (if this can be called democracy) to a representative, orderly and organic form of responsible administration provided with appropriate checks and balances. Protestantism cannot cooperate ecclesiastically with a dictatorship. It must make a clear-cut decision to accept its task of winning America to Christ without any illusion that it has a collaborator in Roman Catholicism.

And it must also rid itself of the illusion that it has an ally in modern culture. The assumption that modern culture has been moving toward a Christian goal has been the undoing of Protestantism. It has weakened its will and confused its faith. Too long has Protestantism stood in awe of modern culture. Its sense of mission has been obfuscated by the messianic pretensions of science, by the prestige of public education, and by the benefits which technology and an ever enlarging state paternalism were conferring upon the people. All these have been accepted by the general community as marks of "progress." And Protestantism has uncritically adopted the popular appraisal, with the result that its own unique responsibility has been obscured and its energies relaxed. A kind of sycophancy toward modern culture has drained off its militant vitality.

It is an amazing fact that for three generations Protestantism stood in awe of this secular culture which we now see in catastrophic ruin. It yielded to it with half its heart, and was thereby rendered incapable of giving wholehearted expression to the Christian faith. It has been afraid to stand up to modern culture, expose its pretensions and proclaim its own gospel. This is because it was half persuaded by these pretensions. Its timidity has been manifested in two types of reaction. I shall call one isolationism, the other appeasement.

A large section of Protestantism has, in effect, withdrawn from the cultural scene and taken its Christianity with it. This reaction into isolation is represented by the conservative or orthodox wing which shades off into fundamentalism. Its constituency cuts across the boundaries of all the denominations. Its isolation, however, has not been a protest against modern culture. On the contrary, conservatism has been totally unaware of the true nature of modern culture. It seemed good, in its own sphere, and this wing of Protestantism adopted a laissez faire attitude toward it. It accepted it, together with its pretensions of "progress," but kept its Christianity apart from it, in another sphere.

Thus, in a kind of cloistered isolation, conservatism has been running on the momentum of the Christian tradition, rather than on the perennial dynamics of the Christian faith. The ideology which Christianity forged for itself in past historical situations has been cherished as definitive and sacrosanct, while the challenge to make Christianity intelligible and potent in the present historical situation has not been recognized.

The other reaction to the modern scene is represented by the liberal wing of Protestantism. Liberalism followed a policy of appeasement. Awed by the formidable character of modern culture in its various forms, especially by the glittering achievements and the messianic hopes of science, and by the development of secular education, liberal Protestantism sensed acutely the relevance of all this to Christianity. But the relevancy which it discerned reflected unfavorably upon Christianity, not upon modern culture.

Liberalism did not propose a radical criticism of this culture in the light of the Christian faith. Instead, it proposed a radical criticism of the Christian faith in the light of modern culture. The question it propounded was: What must Christianity now do to adjust itself to science and to the type of mentality produced by contemporary education? Its major assumption was that the cultural scene represents "progress," while the Christian faith is cluttered with tradition. To make an adjustment, it took over into Christianity the idea of progress as it was secularly conceived, and undertook to insert the Christian ethic of the Kingdom of God into the social process by identifying it with the secular goal.

Thus liberalism played into the hands of secularism by offering it a Christianity which was itself secularized. Its moralism was no escape from secularism, but rather assimilation to it. Its Kingdom of God was merely a translation into religious vocabulary of the utopianism which secularism already possessed. Naturally, those who took the leadership of liberalism have been regarded as the Protestant intelligentsia. Because liberalism seemed able to bring religion and modern culture together, it was identified with breadth of mind, in contrast with the narrower outlook of conservative orthodoxy which dwelt apart, neither penetrated by modern culture nor seeking to penetrate it with the gospel.

The attempt to appease this culture by giving so much of Christianity away to moralism and secularism was sure to find a ready response in certain areas of a mentality produced by a secularized education. But this form of "adjusted Christianity" has been conspicuously sterile. It has lacked power and the sense of urgency that belongs to the Christian faith. It has rested in its negations. It had no dynamic of its own. It expressed itself chiefly in a sigh of intellectual relief when it heard wise men declare that Christianity was just as simple as doing good and that the profundities of the gospel were, after all, virtually meaningless.

In two words, conservatism represents arrested development; liberalism represents decadence. It should be obvious that neither isolation from nor appeasement of modern culture, neither conservative orthodoxy nor liberalism, can win America to the Christian faith. If a choice had to be made between these two, it would probably be easier to rationalize the conservative reaction than the liberal. For conservatism has at least kept alive the conviction that Christianity is true. But it holds its truth in cryptic forms which are opaque, not only to the secular mind, but, I am bound to say, to the mind of conservative Christians themselves. The traditional ideology is used less as an expression of genuine insight, understanding and conviction than as a set of slogans to maintain denominational morale, or around which to rally partisan movements within the denominations or across their boundaries. This emotionalized rallying around orthodox slogans is probably an inevitable, though blind, reaction against the appeasement of modern culture by liberalism in giving away so much of the substance of the Christian faith.

It is high time for Protestantism to be its Christian self, to assert itself, to stand up to modern culture and declare, "Thou ailest here, and here." But the solemn fact is that Protestantism in its present state is not able to do this on a scale commensurate with such a task. It has been standing still for three or four generations while the world around it has been moving farther and farther out of its reach. Protestantism is weak. In its present state it is no match for the secularism which it confronts. It must look within, with honest eyes, examining itself with diagnostic purpose in search of the focal centers of its weakness. When, with an open and honest mind, it turns inward upon itself, it will surely hear the voice of its own conscience saying, "Thou, too, ailest; thou ailest here, and here."

~ VIII ~

PROTESTANTISM, THOU AILEST
HERE, AND HERE!

IN THE PRECEDING chapter, we said that Protestantism must now confront the contemporary American scene as if the Christianization of America depended, under God, upon it alone. This affirmation will be resented by many Protestants. Their resentment, however, only registers the parlous state into which a considerable body of Protestant thought has fallen. It also suggests the place at which to begin our diagnostic search for the focal sources of Protestant weakness and incompetency. This weakness must be cured; but it cannot be cured until its focal sources are exposed. In this and the following three chapters we shall set forth what I believe are the main sources of Protestant weakness.

1. *Protestantism is being victimized by a false tolerance.* There has infiltrated into a considerable section of the Protes-

NOTE.—The title of this chapter is adapted from Matthew Arnold's "Memorial Verses" on the death of Wordsworth. Referring to Goethe, the poet said:

> "He took the suffering human race,
> He read each wound, each weakness clear;
> And struck his finger on the place,
> And said: *Thou ailest here, and here!*"

tant community a conception of Christianity which reduces it to religion in general. The study of comparative religion and the psychology of religion has found certain elements common to all faiths, including Christianity. The easy inference from these "discoveries" is that the particularities of Christianity are not of its essence, but that its essence is in the common elements which it shares with other faiths. Those who hold this view will resent the affirmation that Protestantism must now act as if the Christianization of America depends, under God, upon it alone. The statement will be regarded as arrogant and intolerant. It will be stigmatized as an expression of "religious imperialism." In acting upon it, it will be said, Protestantism would put itself out of step with the movement which is dedicated to cooperation and fellowship among the various faiths in America.

I certainly would deplore any expression of Protestant purpose that would lead to such a result. One of the promising developments in our time is the fellowship and cooperation which has been growing among Protestants, Catholics and Jews. The minor, and what seems like grudging, part taken by Roman Catholics in this movement is no reason why it should not be fostered to whatever limit Catholics are willing to go. Protestants, however, should recognize that they stand in a different position from that of the two other faiths. Numerically, they represent the faith of the overwhelming majority. The plea for tolerance is therefore necessarily directed toward Protestantism alone. Certainly, the Jews are in no position to exercise intolerance; nor are the Catholics as yet. Religious tolerance, in contemporary America, is a one-way street running from Protestantism to Catholicism and Jewry. It makes no sense otherwise.

The ideology of tolerance which has developed in the atmosphere of this interfaith fellowship should be carefully scrutinized. Protestants, being the majority unit, and prompted by the sentiment of *noblesse oblige,* are tempted to take the concept of tolerance as the virtual equivalent of indifference. "Religion is religion; and it makes little difference what your religion is, so long as you live up to it." Protestants who accept this sentimentalism are naturally encouraged by the Jewish unit which, having no hope or purpose to win America to Judaism, asks only for protection against intolerance. "What makes you a good Protestant and you a good Catholic makes me a good Jew," is the dictum in which the Jewish attitude is frequently, consistently and sincerely expressed. No intelligent Catholic, of course, would subscribe to such a statement. But, for obvious reasons, Catholics can allow it go unchallenged in the cordial atmosphere of the three-sided conference for the sake of its salutary effect upon Protestants! The Protestant leaders of this movement carry this sentimentalism back to their churches as a mark of progress in the rapprochement of the three faiths. The effect upon Protestantism is to emasculate its positive faith and undermine its sense of mission.

This so-called "liberal" view should be laid alongside of the theological "liberalism" to which we referred in the previous chapter. Both are forms of appeasement—the one an appeasement of secularist culture, the other an appeasement of non-Protestant faiths. Protestantism can no more give itself away in the one case than in the other without betraying Christianity. The idea that these three religious faiths are fundamentally alike is simply not true. The Jews and the Catholics may derive some practical profit from the prevalence of this sentimentalism among Protestants, but those Protestants who yield to it only bring injury to their own faith. It is high time that this movement should direct its friendly forums toward a consideration of the vital differences which separate the three faiths. If Catholics will not participate, then let the Jews and Protestants, who have far more in common than either has with Catholicism, project such a forum for themselves.

Protestantism needs no exhortation from other faiths to defend the principle of true tolerance. It has fought in the political arena for religious liberty, for the impartiality of the state toward all religious faiths, and will continue to do so. This is true tolerance. It does not set any too well on the Protestant spirit to be exhorted by Catholicism on this point. And Protestantism will strive to foster in its own ranks an enlightened and generous spirit in the presentation of its own faith, that is, a spirit which recognizes the right of others to hold a different faith. This also is true tolerance. But Protestantism needs to be awakened to the fact that it has been subjected to an organized barrage of false tolerance which, among many of its leaders, has enervated its sense of mission and caused its own faith to be watered down into humanitarianism and sentimentalism. In my judgment, this trend in Protestantism spells decadence.

Good will and fine sentiment, expressed in whatever forms, are no answer to the challenge that secularism offers to Protestantism. Secularism is a state of mind, and its mind will not be changed by Protestant good will. It can be changed only by the *truth*. Unless Protestantism intelligently and profoundly believes that, in its Christianity, it has received the truth that will free modern man from the confusion and meaninglessness of a secularized existence, it might as well retire and leave the field to Catholicism and the innumerable cults and theosophies which have arisen, as they always do when a culture has lost its faith.

2. *Protestantism is handicapped by its names.* Its names do not suggest its true character. On the contrary, they obscure and distort it. The name "Protestantism" itself has this effect. It was saddled upon the movement by an irrelevant incident in the early Reformation days. It capitalizes and "freezes" the negative aspect of the Reformation, creating the impression that its essential genius inheres in its protest against the Roman Catholic Church. This of course belies and betrays the profoundly ecumenical spirit in which the Reformation was conceived. "It perpetuates the appearance that Protestants are an aggregation of rebels, critics and iconoclasts and plays into the hands of the Roman Church by fostering its paternalistic attitude, giving countenance to its assumed right to say: 'Some day you will repent and come back.'" (Quoted from a letter I recently received from a layman.)

The name that history has imposed upon Protestantism tends to keep its eyes fixed so narrowly upon a past historical situation that its present historical situation is not fairly envisaged. Moreover, its name has bred in Protestantism a perverse psychology. It tends to keep so ingrained the repugnance with which "Rome and all its works" are regarded that it does not even allow itself to be strong, lest, in the sheer fact of being strong, it would seem to be like Catholicism!

The denominations which comprise the larger part of Protestantism are also handicapped in the same way. Their names are anachronisms, denoting and giving false dignity to issues that long since should have been consigned to limbo. Note a few of them; tarry with each one long enough to grasp what it really means: "Presbyterian," "Congregational," "Episcopal," "Reformed," "Baptist," "Methodist," "Lutheran"—these and other names perpetuate issues and concepts which, though they once seemed important, no longer command respect from a world whose problems lie in a totally different dimension. The titles of these denominations are hardly more than tags on museum pieces, cherished by ecclesiastical connoisseurs whose sense of living reality is obfuscated by antiquarian pride.

I do not wish to suggest that this weakness in Protestant sectarianism lies merely in its unhappy nomenclature. Of course, the *thing* requires attention far more than the name. And, after all, the thing exists even where the name is beyond criticism. Such titles as "Evangelical," "Disciples of Christ," "Friends," "United Brethren," "Church of Christ," and others similarly suggestive of a wider horizon, are, however, belied by the *thing* which these fine names conceal. But the other group of names, together with the negative title which Protestantism itself has to carry, all tend to obscure the ecumenical character of Protestantism, to impede its orientation in the contemporary world, and to inhibit those dynamic forces which a frontal orientation toward a culture gone secular would release.

3. *Protestantism thinks in categories that are too small to express either the richness or the power of the Christian faith.* How could it be otherwise when it is dispersed into more than two hundred sects, each operating as an autonomous self-contained body, and each arrogating to itself all the functions that belong only to the ecumenical church of Christ? The fact, of course, is that Protestantism does not have a chance to do its own thinking. All its thinking is done for it by its denominations. And these denominations are constituted as ecclesiastically self-enclosed compartments. Some of them are relatively large, many are small. But they all jealously maintain their ecclesiastical independence and sovereignty.

No denomination can think in categories large enough to

express the mind of Protestantism, or to envisage, with any degree of realism, the task which contemporary secular America lays upon Protestant Christianity. Nor can a denomination take with more than helpless apprehension the possibility that another faith may overtake and supersede Protestantism in American life. The denominational mind is necessarily narrow, provincial, shortsighted, detached from the total reality. It cannot rise to the eminence from which alone the whole American scene may be envisaged. Its loyalties are inevitably less than ecumenical. The full richness of the Christian faith can therefore find no adequate expression in the "broken lights" of Protestant denominationalism. And the inherent power of the Christian faith can find no adequate implementation for itself in these autonomous and ecclesiastically insulated "churches." It is true that many Protestant leaders are struggling to think in terms of Protestantism as an ecumenical whole. But they are foot-bound by denominational limitations, and their proposals for implementing Protestantism as a whole have to make their way against the tough grain of sectarian pride and self-interest which a denominational system inevitably generates.

None, or only a negligible few, of these denominations would for a moment claim that it alone is *the* church of Christ, and that the winning of America to Protestant Christianity depends upon its triumph over all other Protestant denominations. Virtually all, when confronted directly with the question, will acknowledge that the members of other "churches" are as truly Christians as those of their own "church," and that each of these other "churches" is a genuine part of the church of Christ. This acknowledgment is becoming more and more explicit and cordial, and is finding expression in fraternal comity and in numerous cooperative activities in local communities and in federations, notably the Federal Council of

"Churches." But the continuing ecclesiastical separation of these denominations belies their acknowledgment of the equal status of their sister "churches" in the ecumenical church of Christ. In so far as this acknowledgment is intelligently sincere, it leaves no Christian ground whatever for the continued maintenance of denominations as "churches." What good reason can my denomination give for persisting in an ecclesiastical separation from yours when it acknowledges that yours is a genuine part of the one church of Christ? When the issue is faced in this form, every reason turns to ashes in the mouth as but the petty expression of an unregenerate sectarianism bogged down in its own egotism, pride and inertia.

America will never be won by a sectarianized Protestantism. The modern mind does not regard our sectarianism with mere indifference; it holds it in contempt. There is nothing in Christianity to which the common-sense secular mind reacts with such insufferance as the irrational walled-in divisions which Protestantism maintains. This attitude of the modern mind is not going to change. Protestantism itself must do the changing if it is ever to turn the tide of secularism which has been ebbing away from it. It must present itself as a united whole to the America which it is out to win.

This means that Protestantism must take the ecumenical concept seriously. It must be under no illusion as to what this concept is. An ecumenical Protestantism cannot become a reality in America so long as its denominations maintain themselves as "churches." So far, the ecumenical concept has been adopted only with stiff sectarian reservations. The imperative of a united church has not become a substantive part of Protestant thinking. It hovers over Protestantism and haunts it, but it has not been seized upon with conviction. If and when the concept of the ecumenical church takes hold of the mind of Protestantism, it will spell the end of its denominations as "churches." The ecumenical church and denominational "churches" are mutually contradictory.

4. *Protestantism has never developed a conscience on the unity that is in Christ.* It carries in its tradition certain unitive principles which have prompted leaders to arise from time to time calling for the unity of the church. But they were voices crying in the wilderness, so far as immediate response could be measured. A tendency had set in early in the Reformation which these prophets of unity could not overcome. We might call it, taking a word from biology, the fissiparous tendency— that is, the tendency of a body to split apart and for each part to act as an autonomous and self-sufficient body. This tendency has never met any effective resistance from the Protestant conscience. Indeed, the role which conscience has played in relation to this fissioning process has been, by and large, to sanction it. It is not difficult to understand why.

Protestantism has historically been the champion of intellectual and religious freedom. It has not always practiced this virtue, but its "better nature" could be appealed to to correct its own lapses. It has stood for the right of private interpretation and the right of dissent. The principle of self-criticism and self-correction inheres in its genius. Most of its denominations arose as a criticism of Protestantism in the name of Protestantism. In their origin they illustrate the freedom of the Protestant spirit. But the rise of these denominations illustrates something else in Protestantism, something that is not good, not to be gloried in, and to be condoned, if at all, only by viewing it charitably in a historical perspective. This "something else" was—and still is—the lack of a conscience capable of disciplining freedom.

Discipline is the correlative of freedom. Freedom is never an absolute. It is an evil unless it is disciplined. In Protestantism, this discipline could not, of course, be imposed by an external or arbitrary authority. If there was to be any restraint upon freedom, it had to proceed from conscience whence the assertion of freedom itself arose. The history of Protestantism is tragic in that it never developed a conscience which could discipline its freedom of dissent, and thereby hold its differences within the bounds of the unity that is in Christ. I say it is tragic, because the undisciplined freedom of dissent was used to sanction and foster the fissiparous tendency which has divided Protestantism into innumerable "churches." That is to say, the dissenters carried their freedom beyond the limits prescribed by the spirit of Christ.

The fault, however, was not one-sided. The dissenters were not always, perhaps never, alone responsible for their withdrawal. They were as often withdrawn from, told to go, excommunicated. The fault lay on both sides. It lay in Protestantism itself whose conscience was highly developed on the side of "the liberty of the Christian man," and sadly undeveloped with respect to his duty to maintain "the unity of the spirit in the bond of peace." I am not asserting that such a conscience would have prevented all divisions. That would involve too optimistic an appraisal of human nature even when it was reinforced by as much of the grace of God as human nature is capable of receiving. But I would strongly affirm that the operation of such a conscience would have precluded many a division and, where division occurred, would have left the doors open on both sides of the cleft for an easier reconciliation and reunion.

Modern Protestantism is the heir of the factionalism, the contentiousness, the theological egotism in which its denominations had their origin. It is also the heir of the same lack

31792

of conscience on the unity that inheres in a common allegiance to Christ, the head of the church. Happily, there are signs that such a conscience is being formed. The old, brittle spirit of divisiveness is waning in the more enlightened areas of Protestantism. But it still survives, and few are the denominations that are not profoundly disturbed, at this very moment, by the threat of its resurgence. Though the twentieth century has already seen more mergers of two or more denominations than in the whole history of American Protestantism, it must be sadly recorded that the same period has seen more new sects formed on its periphery than in any equal previous period. The integrative process is matched by at least an equal disintegrative process. The baneful heritage of this fissiparous tendency remains in even the strongest and most enlightened of our denominations. It exists as sectarian inertia, complacency and preoccupation with narrow unecumenical interests. And this when Protestantism faces the stupendous task of winning an America which has been steadily drifting away from it and which only an ecumenical Protestantism can hope to win.

~ IX ~

PROTESTANT LOCALISM

THIS CHAPTER is a continuation of the analytical task begun in the previous chapter where we discussed four focal sources of Protestant weakness. I wish now to consider a fifth and, in the two following chapters, two other sources whose effect is to keep Protestantism from being strong.

5. *Protestantism is weak at its base, namely, its local churches.* Here there appears an ailment for which I shall have to coin a word. I shall call it "localism"—a state of mind in which the local church tends to think of itself as a self-sufficient entity, that is, virtually as an end in itself. This is in contrast with a state of mind in which the local congregation is primarily conscious of itself as the expression in this particular place of the ecumenical church of Christ and the ecumenical Christian faith. (I could have said "catholic," with a small "c," instead of "ecumenical," but to avoid confusion, I have found it necessary to reserve the word "Catholic" to apply to the Roman Catholic Church, even though I, with all Protestants, emphatically reject its claim to catholicity.)

Localism is the ultimate opposite, as denominationalism is the proximate opposite, of ecumenicalism. Localism exists, primarily, because of (1) the decaying significance of the denominations and (2) the non-existence of an ecumenical church to which the local church could transfer the loyalty which it formerly gave to the denomination. A congregation is thus left to its own self-consciousness with no higher ecclesiastical loyalty than is expressed in a lightly held traditional and quite pragmatic connection with its denomination. The local churches of Protestantism are thus in the way of becoming orphaned churches.

Those denominations which call themselves "congregational"—such as the Baptists, Disciples and Congregationalists —contribute directly to this weakness in Protestantism. In their case, localism is the inevitable effect of a thoroughly wrong ecclesiastical theory. This theory sees the local church as the ultimate, independent entity, and the general church, whether denominational or ecumenical, as only the sum of these local autonomous units. Naturally, under such an atomistic conception, the consciousness of the local church would be unduly inflated with self-importance, and its sense of responsibility to the whole body of Christ would be at a minimum.

But those denominations which, historically, have had some awareness of the wholeness of the church of Christ and of every local congregation as the expression in a particular place of this larger church, are hardly less afflicted with localism than are the "congregational" denominations. True, they have probably always recited the clause in the Apostles' Creed, "I believe in the holy catholic church," with slightly more unction than their more congregationally minded neighbors, but the denomination obstructed their vision so that they hardly knew to what the words referred. Their horizon was ecclesiastically limited to the denomination; beyond that their recitation of the creed expressed hardly more than a pious sentiment vaguely directed toward a mystical something commonly called "the church invisible."

But now, in contemporary Protestantism, the significance of all the denominations is in a general process of decay. Both clergy and laity now tend to think of their denomination more as a traditional fellowship and a practical agency than as a living witness to something formerly held to be of great importance and distinctively its own. Thus the local churches of Presbyterian, Methodist, Evangelical Reformed, United Brethren and other denominations of this order, tend to centralize their consciousness, not in the denomination, but in the local congregation. In this respect, they are hardly distinguishable from their outright "congregational" neighbors. The Episcopal and Lutheran denominations also experience this same decay of denominational vitality, but perhaps not so sharply as those I have mentioned.

This localism spells weakness, and it may spell decadence unless a true ecumenicalism comes in to lift the vision and loyalty of local churches to a consciousness of their participation in and allegiance to the whole church of Christ. We shall return to this matter later. For the present, I wish to direct attention to two consequences which flow from this undisciplined, relatively irresponsible, atomistic parochialism.

A congregation in whose consciousness the bond of loyalty to any larger church has been thinned down to a mere traditional or pragmatic connection (whether by the un-Christian theory of "congregationalism" or by the vanishing significance of its denomination) is in danger of drifting either toward secularism or toward some form of religious fanaticism.

(a) Consider first the tendency toward secularism. The scandalous overlapping of Protestant local churches in American society subjects each congregation to a competitive struggle to maintain its existence. In this rivalry, it is humanly inevitable that each such church will appeal to superficial or irrelevant motives in gaining new members. By this I mean motives which fall short of a genuine religious response.

Under such conditions, the act of uniting with the church carries with it hardly more than local implications. It becomes a quite casual matter, based largely on considerations of social affinity or family tradition or the personality of the present minister or the "liberalism" of the preaching or other collateral attractions which a particular congregation offers. Appeal to such motives tends to lower the threshold of church membership to the level of the secular community. It is on a par with one's act in joining the Rotary club, or the Masonic lodge, or the Parent-Teacher association, or any of the numerous uplift organizations in the community. One unites with *this* church, and the act is accompanied with only a minimum of consciousness that one is uniting with *the* church.

This inevitably affects the character of the local church itself. A membership recruited in this way has to be held together by the same motives which recruited it. Thus these motives become institutionalized in forms of entertainment and social activity which have little relevance to the religious life, but do help to maintain the morale of such a church. The result is that these collateral secular activities and attractions tend to overshadow and eclipse the essential religious character of the church. The congregation becomes smug, "clubby" and self-centered. It becomes a class church, in which only those of congenial intellectual or social tastes feel at home. Such a church expresses itself in the appeal to join "this" church because it is *different,* thus minimizing the essential respects in which "this" church is, or ought to be, the *same*—that is, the ecumenical church of Christ at this particular place. The final effect is to inflate the local consciousness and to shrink the ecumenical consciousness.

This process of the secularization of the local church has gone farther than Protestants generally are aware. It manifests itself in the extreme emphasis upon the paramount importance of sociability, of greeting people at the church door, of establishing social relations among the members, new and old—in short, of making everybody "feel at home." The feeling of being at home, however, is not an ecumenical feeling of being at home in the church of Christ, but of belonging to this particular social fellowship. The cultivation of this feeling tends to create in the individual the demand for its satisfaction as the ground on which his membership in the church is to be continued.

In the human nature of the case, not everybody can be made to feel at home in this local sense. So the number of those who give the lack of sociability as their reason for *not* joining a particular church is likely to be as great as the number of those who actually join because of its sociability. How often do we hear the petulant report: "I went to such and such a church and no one spoke to me. I will not go there again."

This demand for local sociability as the basis of church membership and loyalty develops an appetite that grows by what it feeds on. The church, on its part, tends to lose the ecumenical conception of itself and adopts methods of recruiting and maintenance which are little short of coddling. And the individual tends to conceive his church relation as the bestowal of a favor upon the church, rather than as an indispensable means of grace. Thus the very structure of the local church tends to rest upon the whims of its members. It does not evoke in them the sense of awe and reverence and humility which is basic in Christian loyalty. In a word, this overstimulation of sociability tends to destroy religious spontaneity in the individual.

Let any Protestant pastor examine his own routine with the purpose of appraising the quality of his daily labors in keeping his church going and building it up with new accessions to its membership. He will find that he has been engaged in making approaches and appeals that are dishearteningly superficial and trivial. He has not done this of his own accord or because he is unaware of the lack of depth and strength in this method; indeed, he often recoils from this cheapening of his vocation. And he would reproach himself but for one consideration: he *has* to do it! He is driven to it by the practical necessity that is forced upon him in the competitive struggle of local churches in his community.

Vast numbers of Protestant Christians wait inertly to be coddled into a church when they have moved their residence into a new community. They lack religious spontaneity because their past relation to the church has been based, not upon profound religious feeling or conviction, but upon local attractions.

This condition cannot be cured while such competitive Protestantism endures. Until Protestantism finds the will to build in every local community more stately mansions for its soul—more stately in breadth and height and depth than the competitive and wasteful and parochial-minded local churches which now blight while they bless their local communities— it will not deserve to win America, even if it could do so.

It should be unnecessary to say that what I have written is no narrow condemnation of the sociabilities of local church life. From its earliest beginnings the Christian faith has found a positive expression of its fellowship on the common level of social intercourse. I am not piously exhorting the churches to abandon these activities. Nor am I exhorting them to be ecumenical-minded. Such an exhortation would be utterly futile, for they can hardly be expected to be ecumenical-minded so long as the ecumenical faith of Protestantism has no visible and functioning embodiment to which these local churches would organically belong and from which, rather than from themselves, they would draw the substance and sustenance of their spiritual life.

(b) The other tendency of this irresponsible localism manifests itself in the opposite direction. It issues in a sterile religious fanaticism. Lacking any profound consciousness of belonging to an ecumenical Christianity, the local church becomes an easy prey to the purveyors of religious vagaries. These vagaries are too well known, too multifarious and too widely prevalent on the margins of contemporary Protestantism to require any specific listing here. The self-centered, congregationally minded local church has no adequate protection against the nondescript, irresponsible and fanatically minded preacher who thinks he is doing God's service by invading a church with his weird doctrines (always proved by the Bible!) and sowing the seeds of discord and alienation from ecumenical Christianity.

Thousands of these half-orphaned local churches in all parts of the country, and in all save a very few of the denominations, have become victims of this invasion. To call it an invasion is not an exaggeration. It is now assuming the form of an organized attack upon ecumenical Protestantism, and it selects the semi-orphaned local church as the vulnerable point of its attack. Irresponsible schools have lately sprung up like mushrooms overnight and are turning out large numbers of half-baked preachers, intensively indoctrinated with the fantasy or dogma or biblical stereotype which a particular school represents. Wealthy lay men and women, who, as a class, are peculiarly susceptible to the appeal of weird or reactionary interpretations of the Scriptures, provide these schools with liberal financial support.

At least two of the larger denominations—the Baptists and the Disciples—are only now waking up to the fact that in each of them these mushroom schools actually enroll more candidates for the "ministry" than all their educationally responsible seminaries combined. The Presbyterians are not far behind. These and other denominations face the imminent possibility of another division or of a substantial defection.

The local churches of Protestantism are notoriously susceptible to the plausibilities of the nondescript preacher. This is frequently illustrated in the calling of a minister to a vacant pulpit. The manner in which this is done in the "free" local churches of most of our denominations is pathetic to behold— on both the church's side and the minister's. The laity is uninformed concerning the record, the background and the probable trend of a particular candidate's ministry. But it is jealous of its independent prerogative in making the choice. A plausible candidate can easily sweep a congregation off its feet in a single sermon, or he can work his way in by cultivating a faction that is susceptible to his particular brand of biblical interpretation. A congregation may thus unwittingly expose itself to a type of fanaticism whose effect is to alienate it from ecumenical Christianity. Eventually, similarly alienated congregations join in a "movement" whose end is rupture or a substantial defection, leading perhaps to the formation of another denomination or several of them.

Obviously something is wrong here—radically wrong. Does the fault lie with the fundamentalists and the premillennialists and the restorationists and the perfectionists and the pietists and all the other forms of this motley fanaticism? Proximately, yes. Fundamentally, no. The radical fault lies in Protestantism itself. We are only witnessing another exhibition of the spirit which has characterized Protestantism for centuries. It is the identical spirit which founded all our denominations, including those now most enlightened. Protestant history is only repeating itself.

The very denominations which are now threatened with fresh divisions originated on the basis of no less narrow stereotypes of biblical interpretation than those which now disturb their own unity. The continued separate existence of these denominational "churches" is subject to the same judgment as that which they pronounce on the present disturbers of their peace. The long life and the present respectability of these denominations must not obscure this embarrassing fact. The distinctive tenets which are cited as reasons for their continued separate existence are in the same category of narrow fanatical stereotypes as those by which fundamentalism and restorationism and all the rest now threaten further division.

We saw, in the previous chapter, how the fissiparous tendency in Protestantism had historically operated to divide it into a congeries of denominational "churches." This same tendency is now operating to disintegrate these denominations into an amorphous congeries of independent, uncoordinated, parochial-minded local churches. Two or three generations ago, the tenets and practices of each denomination were sufficiently strong to hold its local churches in a vital, even if sectarian, solidarity. But the denominations no longer have the significance or the inner strength they once had. They are, in truth, hardly more than survivals of an era that is past. Few, if any, of the larger bodies hold any distinctive convictions which, if their denominations were not already in existence, would constrain them to start a new denomination today.

The denominational system is becoming increasingly hollow. This fact is at once encouraging and ominous. Encouraging, if it actually represents the emergence of an ecumenical consciousness which transcends the denominational consciousness and thus weakens it. How long these denominational entities can continue as separate "churches" depends upon the strength and vividness of the ecumenical consciousness and the speed with which it can come to grips with the Protestant conscience.

But the decaying significance of these denominations is ominous, because it tends to leave their local churches orphaned, unmothered by any spiritual and vital attachment to any general church beyond their local habitat. The denomination formerly served this purpose, but, having lost so much of its theological, ecclesiastical and spiritual significance, it has been reduced, virtually, to a mere pragmatic agency through which its local churches clear their missionary and benevolent activities. To this agency there still adheres, of course, a certain sentimental attachment based upon tradition, procedural familiarity and special acquaintance among its personnel.

It should be obvious that Protestantism cannot win America unless this disintegrative process now going on within its own body is overcome by an integrative process at the ecumenical level. Indeed, Protestantism cannot even maintain itself as a living force while the significance of its denominational structures is decaying and its local churches are becoming more and more parochial-minded and autonomous. The only hope for the survival of Protestantism, not to mention its winning of America, lies in its becoming organically ecumenical. But this hope must be grasped and implemented before the decay of the denominational structures has gone too far. That is to say, before the tenuous bond that now holds the local churches to some degree of spiritual loyalty has become so weakened by the disintegrative effects of localism that they will have lost the will, and the denomination itself will have lost the corporate strength, required to carry them into an organically ecumenical Protestantism.

The blight of localism spreads through the whole of Protestantism like an endemic disease. Its modern symptoms are secularism and fanaticism. But its historical symptoms still persist in the very denominations whose leaders, with sublime inconsistency, wring their hands before the ravages of its contemporary manifestation. The cure of this disease will require heroic treatment. Indeed, it calls for a profound revolution in the consciousness of Protestantism and in its implementation. Until Protestantism becomes conscious of itself as a whole, and embodies its unity in a form competent to evoke a positive ecumenical consciousness and an ecumenical allegiance on the part of its local churches, these churches will continue to gravitate toward secularism or will be the prey of any preacher of fantastic and fanatical doctrines who comes along.

The decay of denominational significance thus makes possible today an ecumenical Protestantism which was not possible at any earlier period. But it is also a solemn warning that, if the disintegrative process represented by the increasing parochialism of the local churches continues, the achievement of such a possibility will be even more difficult than it would have been in the heyday of sectarian pride and conflict. I see only two alternatives. One is for Protestantism blindly to allow itself to disintegrate into a congeries of local churches, each one an easy victim of either secularism or fanaticism. The other is for Protestantism to discover the inherent but hidden ecumenical genius of the Reformation and to implement itself as an organic empirical entity within whose mothering embrace each local church may find its true dignity as the expression of the ecumenical church of Christ in this particular place. The latter, I affirm, is the only adequately Christian way in which the relationship of a local church to the body of Christ may be conceived.

Such a profound reformation of Protestantism requires, fundamentally, one thing only. It is that Jesus Christ shall be given his true place as the sole authority in the church of which he is the living Head. But Protestantism will not do this so long as the Bible continues to be accorded the place which belongs only to Christ. This most fundamental source of Protestant weakness will be discussed after we have made an examination of the manner in which Protestantism wastes its resources.

~ X ~

THE WASTED POWER OF PROTESTANTISM

POTENTIALLY, Protestantism is enormously strong; actually, it is pathetically weak. It is not weak in the sense that it lacks either the spiritual or material resources to win America to the Christian faith. Its weakness is relative to its great strength and is to be measured by contrast with its strength. Protestantism is weak because it does not use its strength; it lacks the will to use it. It huddles in sectarian ecclesiasticisms each of which calls itself a "church" and acts as a church, arrogating to itself all the functions and prerogatives of the ecumenical church of Christ. Its strength is not brought to bear in a total impact upon American mentality, which is now shaped into mass molds by a relatively few huge blocs of secular interest. Protestantism in its present state is no match for this America.

So long as its denominations continue to function as autonomous "churches," Protestantism cannot command the public respect which its enormous potential resources and the dignity of the Christian religion should command. Its fragmented and atomized ecclesiasticisms are helpless before the solidarities in which the secular interests of contemporary life now mold

114

American mentality. These denominational "churches" evoke hardly more than a polite gesture of respect from the community. The public in general takes condescending note of their "sincerity" but is not impressed by the religion they profess to represent. This courteous condescension of the local and national community toward the denominational "churches" ought at least to gripe the pride of Protestantism if it does not stab its conscience wide awake. Let us, then, add a sixth source of weakness in Protestantism to the list previously discussed.

6. *Protestantism has lacked the will to be strong.* It has even cultivated a perverse psychology which makes a virtue of weakness. Because it sees Catholicism possessed of a wrong kind of power, a power that is essentially evil and incompatible with both Christianity and democracy, Protestantism pretends to shrink from the right kind of power and takes refuge in a pious rationalization of weakness. It lulls itself into complacency by intoning such texts of Scripture as: "Not by might nor by power, but by my spirit, saith the Lord," interpreting this as God's sanction of weakness in the human organs upon which even He must depend for the triumph of his Spirit. This interpretation has always comforted the denominations, big and little, in their huddling separatism.

And yet, paradoxically, every denominational "church" is ambitious to be as strong as it can! And as it grows stronger it is none too modest in letting the world know how strong it is. I suppose that there is not a single denomination that would not rejoice if its own growth should so far surpass all other denominations that it eventually became the whole of Protestantism—as Aaron's rod swallowed up all the rods of the sorcerers before Pharaoh. From Protestantism's becoming strong in this manner, no denomination would shrink! But it piously pretends to shrink from allowing Protestantism to become strong in any other manner. Every attempt to release the strength which Protestantism potentially possesses has to go against the tough grain of this perverted psychology.

There is a touch of the pusillanimous about this. It is a form of escapism—an escape from responsibility. Wherever there is power there is responsibility. The two are inseparably correlative, and each is the measure of the other. Strength is not an evil in itself. To shrink from being strong is to shrink from responsibility. To shrink from responsibility is cowardice. The responsibility that rests upon Protestantism, under God, is to win America to the Christian faith. Its responsibility inheres in the concrete fact that it has the power to discharge it. It cannot evade this responsibility by harking back to the new-born church of New Testament times. Nor can it discharge its responsibility by a slavish attempt to reproduce the forms assumed by that infant church in an ancient society.

Protestantism is a grown-up church. It lives in a highly complex society whose mentality is molded by large blocs of mass secular interest. Each bloc represents power. This America can be reached only by a religion that is able to penetrate the collective system which fashions individual mentality, to reform its evils and to cooperate with it where it is good. In the degree that Protestantism accepts its responsibility for the character of American civilization, it must accept and exercise the right kind of strength necessary to discharge it. Catholicism is aware of this bloc structure of American psychology and is dealing with it in ways that accord with its own genius. Protestantism is not even aware of it, or only dimly so. The myopic vision of its sectarian "churches" is preoccupied with obsolete issues, individualistic methods and worn-out denominational structures, all of which taken together spell impotence.

But Protestantism can discharge this responsibility only if it can be bombed out of the inertia of its sectarianism and, with God's help, create for itself a democratically based solidarity of fellowship in a unity of structure competent to match the magnitudes of secularism which constitute its total environment. It has the resources to win America if it will but release and mobilize them.

Protestantism is, numerically, far and away the ascendant religious faith in American society. Despite the enormous increase in the membership of the Roman Catholic Church, due primarily to the immigration of millions of new citizens from Catholic countries before immigration was restricted, and to a high birth rate, Protestantism still outnumbers it by more than two to one. The latest statistics show a Protestant membership of 43,000,000 and a Catholic membership of 23,000,000. But many Protestant churches do not include baptized infants in their statistics, while Catholics do. The *Year Book of American Churches* estimates the adult membership (over thirteen years of age) of Protestant and Catholic churches at more than 37,000,000 and 17,000,000, respectively. I believe the Protestant adult membership is nearer 40,000,000.

Not to be overlooked in this inventory of numerical strength is the wide populational periphery surrounding the Protestant churches, including multimillions whose predilection for Protestantism is, of course, not registered in the statistics of church membership. In this periphery is represented, in large measure, the apostasy from Protestantism to secularism. Though these millions are indifferent to religion and add nothing directly to the strength of the church, they constitute, nevertheless, a sentimental asset for Protestantism. Catholicism has no comparable periphery; virtually its entire numerical strength is represented in its actual membership.

The preponderant numbers of Protestantism are not a measure of its actual strength, but rather an exposure of its weakness. These millions of church members have no unity of action, not even a unity of purpose. Protestants deceive themselves when they sing, "Like a mighty army moves the church of God; we are not divided; all one body we." They are divided; they are not one body; they are anything but a mighty army. The value of the numerical statistics lies in their revelation of the *potential* strength of Protestantism—what Protestantism could be if it would, if it had the will to accept its responsibility and undertook, in faith and freedom, to discharge it.

In addition to its numerical strength, American Protestantism is enormously wealthy. Statistics are not available showing the total wealth of its membership. But it is safe to assume that the income of its 43,000,000 members represents, conservatively, one-third of the total income of the nation's 139,000,000 population. This assumption is fully warranted by the fact that Protestant strength is found chiefly in the middle and upper income brackets. The numerical strength of Catholicism is preponderantly represented in the lower income brackets. But Protestantism is very rich. If its nearly one-third of the total population received one-third of the total national income of $125 billion in 1944, its members received over $41 billion.

How much of this income was given to the support of their churches? It was a very large amount. Here again the figures for the whole of Protestantism are not available. But the *Year Book of American Churches* has published the amounts given to church work by nineteen denominations. The total giving of these nineteen bodies for 1944 was $423,695,471, or an average per capita of $16.57. This per capita average is, no doubt, fairly representative of the whole of Protestantism. On the basis of this per capita average, the total gifts of Protestants to the work of their churches amounted in 1944 to $711,510,-000. Let us take a conservative figure and say $700,000,000.

From this point on, I hope especially to arrest the attention of the laity. They are the givers of this $700,000,000. I am not concerned to moralize on the question whether their giving should be considered generous or niggardly. I am concerned only with the fact that it adds up to a tremendous sum of money. How was this huge sum spent? Every layman ought to be informed on the distribution of his and his church's gifts. The Catholic layman is not informed on such matters. All knowledge of the financing of the Roman Church is kept strictly within the most inner circle of the hierarchy. No accounting is ever given to the laity or the public. Protestantism could not tolerate such a system, and public policy in democratic America should not tolerate it in Catholicism or in any organization, secular or religious, which receives and spends voluntary contributions.

In Protestantism, there is no secrecy. All its books are open to the laity and the public. The receipts and detailed expenditures are audited by public accountants and published. The layman can have every assurance that his gifts are spent with meticulous care by the consecrated men and women to whom the local church or the denomination commits the administration of its affairs. It is not the administration of church funds that the layman needs to call in question, but *the system that is being administered*—this he ought to think about, and seriously.

Let us, for a moment, return to statistics. The Roman Catholic Church has 14,791 local churches in this country. Protestantism has 230,000 local churches. The average layman and even the average minister will read this statistical fact with a touch of pride. "I did not realize," he is likely to say, "that Protestantism was that much stronger than Catholicism. We have, then, 17½ times as many churches as Catholicism. Wonderful! Catholicism has a long way to go to catch up with us Protestants." If I dared to speak as St. Paul spoke, I would say, "Thou fool!" These figures do not indicate Protestant strength. They expose Protestant weakness.

Protestantism, with only twice the Catholic membership, supports 17½ times as many local churches. There would be occasion for satisfaction if there were as many as 230,000 cities, towns and villages in the length and breadth of this great country, and if these 230,000 Protestant churches were distributed among them all. But this is notoriously not the case. Nearly all these churches exist side by side with other Protestant churches in small and large communities. They are not there because the community needs them, nor because Protestantism needs them, nor because Christianity needs them. They are there because each one of more than two hundred denominational "churches" imagines that its peculiar brand of Protestantism ought to be propagated by the organization and maintenance of its own local churches regardless of the effect upon these communities and upon Protestant Christianity as a whole.

Now I ask the layman: Does he honestly want to give his money for that kind of thing? Can he honestly say that the peculiarities of his denomination mean so much to the Kingdom of God that he takes pride in its invasion of a community already overchurched, or that he takes pride in continuing to

maintain it in his own community at the cost of continuing
the division of Christianity in his community into little fragments of Protestantism? That is what the layman is now doing.
That is where his money goes. Most of the $700,000,000
annually given by the Protestant laity goes to the support of
this system—a system which, let it spawn as many of these
churches as it will, only makes Protestantism that much weaker.

Consider how this $700,000,000 a year was spent. Eighty
per cent, or $560,000,000, was spent on the upkeep of these
local churches. The remaining 20 per cent, or $140,000,000,
went for "benevolences," that is, for all purposes other than
the expenses of the local church.

Look first at the local church category, whose budget is
$560,000,000 a year. There is scarcely a town or village in
the United States that is not scandalously overchurched. Four,
five and six Protestant churches in little villages and towns of
less than 1,000 inhabitants. Fourteen and even twenty churches
in the typical county seat small town. Thirty and forty churches
in small cities of 20,000 and 50,000 inhabitants. Fifty and
sixty churches in cities with a population of 100,000 and 200,-
000—and so on up to the largest cities, where every one of
Protestantism's 230 denominations is likely to be represented
by from two to one hundred local churches each.

Does the layman like this picture? He gives $560,000,000
a year to produce it. Is he aware of its implications? Probably
not. He is caught in the inertia of the denominational system;
he is told that his denominational "church" represents the
"true form of New Testament Christianity" and that "loyalty
to the Bible" requires that it shall have a church in as many
communities as it can invade. He does not see what this
policy, pursued by all the other denominations, each of which
imagines that it, too, represents the "true form of New Testa-

ment Christianity," does to Protestantism and to Christianity itself. And so he pays $560,000,000 a year for the upkeep of local churches, fully two-thirds of which, including most probably the one of which he is himself a member, are not only supernumerary but an enfeeblement of the cause of Christ.

Any discussion of this subject addressed to the layman is admittedly delicate. I am not suggesting that he should suddenly withdraw the support he now gives to his local church. Such a suggestion would be little short of wanton. Protestantism has these churches on its hands. They are a tremendous drag on Protestantism, a scandal in the eyes of the world and an affront to Christ, who deserves a more worthy institutional embodiment in every community than any denominational local church can give him. But these churches are the bearers of something immeasurably precious—that is, Protestant Christianity itself. Protestantism exists within these churches. It has no other habitation—this is its sorry fate. And this is the sorry fate of the layman—he has no present Christian alternative but to support them.

Nevertheless, the intelligent laity who give their millions to the support of Protestant local churches have grounds for a revolt—only they must be sure that their revolt is directed at the real cause of their discontent. The real cause is not these local churches, but *the system that keeps them separate,* under the delusion that the denomination which each represents is "the true New Testament church." Against this system and the delusion that sustains it I affirm, with an untroubled conscience, that the time has come for the laity to revolt.

In encouraging such a revolt against a system that spawns probably three times as many local churches as Protestantism needs, that keeps these local churches weak and keeps Protestantism weak, I do not intend to tell the layman that by cutting off this great economic waste he could save money! A strong Protestantism will cost as much money as a weak and wasteful Protestantism, and perhaps more. But it will be money productively spent, under a substantially curtailed overhead, and on missionary, educational, evangelistic and social enterprises competent to challenge the formidable secularism of our time.

We have been considering the huge amount of money which the Protestant layman gives for the upkeep of denominational local churches. This is where 80 per cent of his giving goes. We must now look briefly at the 20 per cent which goes to benevolences, that is, for all purposes other than the upkeep of the local churches. This amounts to $140,000,000 a year. It is spent on home and foreign missions, religious education, various philanthropies, denominational overhead and a niggardly pittance on interdenominational work. The philanthropic, educational and interdenominational expenditures are, no doubt, self-justifying. But the layman would do well to look into denominational overhead and missions.

Every one of the 230 Protestant denominations maintains a central headquarters; perhaps 100 of them maintain regional and/or state headquarters; and at least 50 of them maintain metropolitan headquarters in the larger cities of the country. These various headquarters are manned by a veritable army of bishops, presidents, secretaries of missionary, educational and benevolent departments, superintendents, editors, researchers, clerks, stenographers. Every one of these functionaries is essential to the administration of the affairs of the denomination. They are paid a scale of salaries so modest that the layman would be ashamed to operate his business upon it. The layman can be assured that denominational funds are handled, not only wisely, but with meticulous care and parsimony. It is not their administration, but the sectarian system to which the layman's attention is directed—a system that requires these completely outfitted headquarters for each one of these 230 denominations.

Manifestly, from the point of view of Protestantism as a whole, there is an enormous waste in the overlapping of all this overhead. I venture to assert that a united Protestantism could administer the present activities of these denominations on an overhead budget not much larger than that which the Methodist Church alone now requires. If this statement seems too extreme, we could add the overhead budget of the Presbyterian Church to that of the Methodist, and safely say that the amount spent on the overhead of the remaining 228 denominations is a waste of the Lord's money. If we confine our observations to the 49 denominations having 50,000 or more members each, and constituting more than 90 per cent of Protestantism's total membership, our conclusion would be that the amount spent on the overhead of 47 of them is economic waste, from the standpoint of Protestantism as a whole. Does the layman like this picture?

However, he has yet to look under the overhead and ask how and for what the great bulk of this $140,000,000 in the category of "benevolences" is expended. It is chiefly spent on foreign and home missions, than which there is no more sacred enterprise of the church of Christ. And it is wisely and economically spent, so far as its executive administration is concerned. But it is spent for the extension of the denominational system in America and in foreign lands. Is the layman duly conscious of this aspect of the missionary enterprise when he makes his gift? Probably not. He gives his money to missions with the single thought that he is helping to spread the gospel at home and abroad, as indeed he is. This central reality in the missionary enterprise must not be clouded, nor its motivation weakened, by the inquiry upon which we are engaged.

But the intelligent layman is competent to consider whether he really desires the gospel to be spread in the forms of Protestant sectarianism. He can weigh such a question without weakening his basic motive in supporting the cause of missions as such. Does he really desire to transplant our American denominations to China and India and Japan and Africa and the rest of the non-Christian world—these denominations which are in a process of decaying significance at home and which have no meaning at all in foreign lands? The missionaries do not want them transplanted. They are hobbled by their denominational constraints. The people to whom they bring the gospel are confused and bewildered by them. The missionaries of all our more enlightened denominations are protesting against the necessity of operating in this sectarian framework. On every occasion, they speak almost as one voice, pleading for an ecumenical Protestantism at home so that they can carry an ecumenical Christian gospel and establish only an ecumenical church abroad.

I do not wish to overemphasize the economic waste in the sectarian administration of the missionary enterprise, though it deserves strong emphasis. But the spiritual or Christian imperative which the missionaries and the young churches in mission lands lay upon American Protestantism to administer the missionary enterprise ecumenically is so manifest that it dwarfs all other considerations.

The expenditures for home missions—that is, the extension of denominational churches in the United States—should be subjected to the same examination as we have suggested in the case of foreign missions. Of the annual $140,000,000 given by the Protestant churches to "benevolences," the proportion allocated to home missions varies in the various denominations. In some it is larger, in others less, than the foreign missions budget. But in each denomination it is a substantial amount. The economic waste involved in the maintenance of 230 separate denominational agencies for the administration of home missions is the same, in effect, if not in amount, as in the case of foreign missions. But here, too, the Christian imperative for an ecumenical administration far transcends in importance the economic waste involved in its sectarian administration, though this also deserves emphasis.

In examining home missions we are thrown back to a further consideration of local churches; for the chief function of home missions is to establish and maintain local churches in communities where the denomination is not yet represented. All the considerations involved in our previous discussion of local churches in general apply here. Upon the home mission enterprise rests the responsibility of having largely created the unconscionable overlapping and competitive condition of Protestant churches in the now settled communities of the land. These churches were, in large numbers, fostered and sustained by home mission money until they became self-supporting. Each denomination still carries on in the same way, but with a slight difference.

The enlightened leaders of Protestantism are becoming aware of the reproach that falls upon Christianity by the competitive presence of these supernumerary churches in local communities. Steps have been taken to bring the home mission activities of the various denominations into some kind of accord under a policy of courtesy or mutual forbearance—so-called "comity"—in the allocation of new communities to this or that denomination. For example, if the Methodists will agree to leave this new community to the Presbyterians, the

Presbyterians will leave that other new community to the Methodists. This principle of "comity" deserves every encouragement. At best, however, it has only a marginal and temporizing application. It leaves untouched the older communities which the denominations previously invaded with utter disregard of the welfare of Protestantism as a whole. And it leaves these new churches in new communities saddled with the incubus of their sectarian connection and character.

That the laity, by and large, sense the folly of the denominational system has been proved in some 2,500 local communities where so-called "community churches" have been organized, mostly within the past generation. This movement could quite accurately be called a laymen's revolt. It is inspired, negatively, by their disillusionment with denominationalism and by the desire to keep the denominations out, and positively, by the aspiration for a local church embodying ecumenical Christianity. The tragedy of these churches is that there exists no inclusive ecumenical Protestant church to mother them, to which they could give their allegiance. The result is that they have to carry on as orphan churches, or establish some tenuous connection with one of the denominations. In either case, they are unhappily conscious of their nondescript status. Their predicament is at last arresting the attention of Protestant leaders who are cooperating with their leaders to find a solution which will not drive them back into the denominational system.

A further proof of discontent among the laity is found in the numerous mergers of two existing local churches of different denominations in a sort of local federal union which preserves a connection with both denominations. Such mergers are usually prompted by laymen. These mergers represent the same ecumenical aspiration that informs the community church. But they, too, lack the consciousness of *belonging*, a lack which is only intensified by their "belonging" to two different denominations instead of one. What they pathetically long for, though their longing may be inarticulate, is to be integrated in an ecumenical Protestantism which transcends all denominational "churches" and which, as an ecclesiastical mother, would save them from the blight of localism on the one hand and an amphibian division of denominational loyalty on the other.

I cannot express too strongly my belief that the laity of Protestantism, by and large, are profoundly dissatisfied with the sectarian order which constricts their faith, their fellowship and their mission in narrow, exclusive and increasingly meaningless denominational "churches." No message evokes from an assemblage of laymen so ardent a response as does the call for a united Protestantism. This is true in every part of the country and in every denomination, including the most conservative and traditional-minded. In their hearts, Protestant Christians are ecumenical, not sectarian. They want to see a strong Protestantism come into existence. Even among the most denomination-conscious groups, such as the Southern Baptists and the Episcopalians, a visiting speaker on this theme, representing another denomination, finds himself lured into unintended frankness by the hearty response to his message calling for an ecumenical Protestantism.

Surely Protestantism is not permanently condemned to the fate which now holds it in the bondage of sectarian impotence. Is there no hope that its leaders—its parish clergy, its bishops, its huge secretariat, its theologians, its editors of denominational organs—will free themselves from the narrow limitations of an official headquarters mentality and look out upon Protestantism as a whole? These leaders could make articulate the yearning in the hearts of the laity for an ecumenical Protestantism. Instead of devoting themselves to the conjuring up of reasons why an ecumenical Protestantism is impossible, should not the reasons that make its achievement imperative spur them to find the way? There is a way. There must be a way. And Protestantism, if it is to win America, must find it.

~ XI ~

PROTESTANT MISUSE OF THE BIBLE

IN THIS CHAPTER, we bring to a conclusion our analysis of the sources of weakness in Protestantism. In the three preceding chapters we have considered six such sources. I wish now to add one more, which I believe to be fundamental to, if not the root cause of, all the others.

7. *Protestantism is bedeviled by its unscriptural use of the Scriptures.* It has put the Bible in the wrong place—in an unbiblical place; that is, a place it does not claim for itself, but rather condemns. It has put it in the place which Christianity accords to Jesus Christ alone. A false biblicism is, I believe, the root source of Protestant weakness.

The reformers, reacting violently against the Roman Catholic system with the pope at its head, were unwisely led to assume that it was necessary to set up an authority other than Christ himself which would unite Protestantism as Catholicism was united under the papacy. The Bible, newly translated into the vernacular and made available to the laity by the invention of printing, became this authority. It was to be the supreme tribunal of appeal. "The Bible and the Bible alone," said Chillingworth, in an oft quoted dictum, "is the religion of Protestants."

The assumption that the Bible would unify Protestantism early proved to be a delusion. The conference of Luther and Zwingli at Marburg, the intention of which was to unify the German and Swiss reformations, broke down in an unhappy temper over the failure of the two leaders to agree on the interpretation of a single biblical text: "This is my body." From that day on, the misuse of the Bible has vitiated the spirit of Protestantism, narrowed its vision, preoccupied it with petty contention, unendingly divided it into sects, and warped the sublime character of the Bible itself.

The founders of all our denominations claimed the authority of the Bible for their separatist creeds, polities and practices. Obviously, such a result should be the proof that the Bible is not an authority of this kind, for, when it is thus used, it speaks contradictory things to different, but equally devout, readers. A conception and use of the Bible that has broken the church into fragments, each claiming it as the authority for its separate existence, is manifestly false. Any attempt, now, to reunite these fragments on the basis of the authority of the Bible is as fatuous as its success would be hopelessly impermanent.

Yet the whole contemporary movement for the unity of the church—the ecumenical movement—is frustrated by this unscriptural use of the Scriptures. The fundamental debate within this movement is between those who hold the authority of the Bible to be supreme and those who wish to include also the authority of tradition. It is passing strange that in this debate no voice is raised for Jesus Christ as the sole and sufficient authority, supreme over both Bible and tradition. So the ecumenical movement tends to bog down in the impossible attempt to find the basis of unity in legalistic and doctrinal standards derived from either the Bible or tradition or both. American Protestantism in general takes the side of the Bible in this debate. But the history of Protestantism is proof that the quest for unity in the church of Christ on the assumption that the Bible is to be its basis can end only in a blind alley. Protestantism cannot achieve the strength necessary to win America if it continues to stultify itself by clinging to an illusion which has wrought havoc and disunion from the beginning.

At its outset, the Reformation intended to make, and believed it was making, Christ the true and only authority in the church. And contemporary Protestantism will readily affirm on its own behalf that its supreme loyalty is given to him. But this profession has a hollow ring when it is tested by the actual behavior of both historical and contemporary Protestantism. For the truth is that Protestantism has divided its loyalty between Christ and the Bible, and has given the major weight of its loyalty to the authority of the Bible at the expense of its loyalty to Christ. It has misused the Bible in such a manner that the Book has come between Christian faith and the Author and Perfecter of the faith. It has not beheld him face to face with consistent perception, attention, imagination and devotion. Its vision of him has been obscured by its variegated interpretations of the Bible.

In this respect Protestantism has taken the same line as Roman Catholicism. Like Rome, it has insisted that Christ needs an official and authoritative interpreter. For this function, the Roman Church sets up the pope, and Protestantism sets up the Bible. Each, respectively, regards its interpreter as the "vicegerent of Christ on earth," though Protestantism has not been candid enough to use the repugnant words of this Roman Catholic appellation.

It is not generally recognized that the Reformation, in its initial emergence, was vividly conscious of the tension between the authority of the Bible and the authority of Christ. Martin Luther clung tenaciously to the authority of Christ and was profoundly apprehensive lest a misuse of the Bible would derogate from Christ's authority. He held a conception of the Bible that protected him personally from this danger. For Luther, Christ himself was the Word of God, disclosed, to be sure, in the Scriptures, but never to be supplanted by the Scriptures.

However, the clamor for a visible authority to which the divers and divergent opinions arising in the newborn Protestant movement could be referred and judged, overcame his scruples, and his thought fell into the biblical pattern already set by the "radicals" who attached themselves to his reformation, and by the more thoroughgoing biblicism which characterized the Swiss reformation. But at the beginning, Luther felt no need of any other authority to preserve the unity of the Reformation than the authority of Christ. He would have been content, as the late Professor A. C. McGiffert has shown,

to do without any definite authority beyond his doctrine of the forgiving love of God in Christ. That seemed to him adequate for every emergency. But gradually, under the pressure of the radicals on the one side and of the conservatives on the other, he was led to identify his gospel of the forgiving love of God in Christ, which he had always called the Word of God, with the Scriptures, and to find in them the ultimate authority for Christian truth.*

Nevertheless, Luther tried manfully to maintain some sort of balance between the authority of the Scriptures and the author-

* *The Problem of Christian Unity,* by various writers (Macmillan Co., 1921), pp. 40-41.

ity of Christ. And he always weighted the balance on the side
of Christ. Engaged in endless disputation with "adversaries" in
his own camp, he struggled with this issue as no Protestant
leader since his day has struggled with it. In 1535, he wrote:
"When our opponents urge the Scriptures against Christ, we
urge Christ against the Scriptures." He affirmed that "Scripture must not be understood *against* Christ, but *for* Christ.
Therefore, the Scripture must be referred to Christ [that is, for
his judgment or approval] or one cannot claim it as true
Scripture."*

In a magnificent dictum, summing it all up, Luther declared,
"I urge [insist upon] Christ, the Lord, who is Lord [*rex*] also
of the Scriptures." The freedom of the Christian man from
any slavish bibliolatry was evidenced in the view he held of
the Epistle of James, which he called an "epistle of straw"
because it seemed to him—mistakenly, as is generally admitted
—to support the Roman Catholic doctrine of "works of merit"
in opposition to the rest of the New Testament.

We shall not understand Luther's position on the question
of the authority of the Bible versus the authority of Christ, a
position which he never forsook, unless we clearly grasp his
conception of Christ himself as *the Word of God*. The Word
of God was not the letter of the Scripture, nor even the Scripture itself, but that supreme Person whom the Scripture unveils
to the devout reader of its pages. And Christ then, in turn,
becomes the judge of the Scripture. This conception Luther
once expressed in a quaint but apt metaphor by saying that
the Bible is "the cradle of Christ," meaning that it contains
him, unveils him and, at the same time, releases him into his

* *Martin Luther's Works* (Weimar ed.), Vol. 39, I. *Disputations*,
p. 47.

own sovereign, self-authenticating supremacy over the heart of man, over the church and over the Bible itself.*

Outside of Lutheranism, this conception of the Bible has not taken hold of Protestant intelligence. And Lutheranism historically fell into the very literalism and legalism which Luther feared would result from the failure to distinguish between the Word of God and the Scriptures. The distinction is difficult to formulate, and more difficult to communicate, but it is of profound importance. It is one of those fine distinctions which, to the casual observer, seem academic and barren, but, nevertheless, have far-reaching consequences. A church that looks to the Scriptures as the Word of God will be one kind of church. A church that looks to Christ alone as the Word of God will be another and very different kind of church.

American Protestantism is quite unfamiliar with this distinction. It is the heir of the stiff, textual, literalistic and legalistic biblicism of John Calvin, who, so far as I know, never felt the tension between these two authorities as Luther felt it. Calvin was educated in the law, and he interpreted the Bible as if it were a book of law, of divine law, infallibly and equally authoritative in all its parts and in every word. For him, the Bible was itself the divine revelation; it was the Word of God. It was Calvin's type of biblicism that was carried from

---

* It is not my intention to say or imply that the position Luther struggled to maintain is fully satisfactory and final, but only that, if it had prevailed, it would have provided Protestantism with a commanding principle of unity and held in check the tendency toward sectarian divisions "based on the Bible." I cannot subscribe to the concept that Christ is "in the Bible." He is not found in a book. He is to be found *where the Book says he is to be found,* namely, in the living community of believers from which he has never withdrawn his living presence. For further discussion of this subject, see my book, *What Is Christianity?,* especially the chapters on "The Body of Christ" and "The Heresy of Protestantism."

Geneva to western Europe, to England and Scotland, and to North America. American Protestantism has reflected in its sectarianism the Calvinistic view of the Bible, as Continental sectarianism has reflected the lapse of Lutheranism from the high, spiritual Christological ground on which, at the beginning, Luther sought to establish the Reformation.

Luther's compromise at this crucial point had tragic consequences for Protestantism. His compromise and Calvin's outright literalistic biblicism have caused Protestantism to be afflicted with a divided mind in respect to its primary allegiance. It has been a victim of a kind of theological schizophrenia which caused it to vibrate between two authorities. Professing loyalty to Christ, it has been tethered and hamstrung by its literalistic conception of the Scriptures as authoritative. Protestantism has, therefore, not been able to move out into the liberty wherewith Christ has made his church free.

In the degree in which attention is focused upon the Bible as the authority, the authority of Christ is bound to be eclipsed. The Protestant mind has not allowed Christ to be the interpreter of the Bible; it has used the Bible as a legalistic and literalistic interpreter of Christ. Given the right of private interpretation, each individual reader of the Bible, his eyes glued upon the literal text, could affirm: "*This* is what the Bible says," without ever lifting his eyes to Christ, asking him whether this is what he requires or whether it is consonant with his mind. To assume that Christ requires his church slavishly to copy everything in the Bible is to make Christianity a babel of tongues, not to say a babbler of foolishness.

Consider a few of the strange doctrines, the fantastic notions, the weird practices which have been digged out of the Bible and used as stereotyped fixations in the interpretation of the whole book. Exclusive psalm singing, anti-instrumental music in worship, anti-organization for missionary work, pre- or post-millennialism, the second coming of Christ (even the date repeatedly fixed by weird manipulation of the texts in Daniel and Revelation), perfectionism, footwashing, trine immersion, hooks and eyes versus buttons, beards, two-seed-in-the-spirit Calvinism—these are only samples of the innumerable progeny of sanctified trivialities which the false use of the Bible has spawned on the margins of Protestantism.

But no apologist for any denomination may throw a stone of criticism at any of these "queer" interpretations. For he, too, lives in a glass house. The list of vagaries and trivialities is not by any means exhausted by what we find on the margins. It runs through the whole body of Protestantism and takes in every one of its denominations, even the most respectable. It includes their sectarian creeds, their divergent polities, their conflicting views of the ministry, of baptism and the Lord's Supper. It includes episcopalianism versus presbyterianism versus congregationalism versus Quakerism and versus many shadings and modifications of these typical forms of church order and government. These all rest upon scriptural authority! They reflect in the most enlightened areas of Protestantism the vitiating and divisive consequences of the unscriptural use of the Scriptures.

Any use of the Bible which divides Christ's body must be *ipso facto* false to him. The notion that he delegated his authority to a book, or to the writers of a book, for the legalistic regulation of his church, has no basis in fact. And it results in belittling and demeaning Christ. How can anyone who has been fairly confronted by Jesus Christ imagine that he who swept all ecclesiastical literalisms and legalisms aside, thereafter invested a book with authority to set them up again?

His authority deals with vaster issues than these, issues that lie in a totally different dimension. And he has left his church free to use its consecrated intelligence to organize its faith, its worship and its mission in forms that are compatible with his spirit and that promise the fullest expression of his living presence in the church.

It is strange that the irony of this delusion that the authority of the Bible is the basis of unity in the church has escaped the serious consideration of Protestant intelligence. Strange, too, that it has not been discerned how such misuse of the Bible dethrones Christ. Note carefully: I do not say that the Bible dethrones Christ. On the contrary, it bears witness that Christ alone is the Head of his church. It is the misuse of the Bible that dethrones him.

Nowhere does the Bible claim to be an authority above Christ or upon which his authority depends. Its Old Testament looks forward to him. Its New Testament bears witness to his life, teaching, death and resurrection; in factual account, in poetic vision and in discursive interpretation. The Bible is not the source of our faith, or the ground of it, or the proof of it. Christ alone is the source, the ground and the proof of our faith. The Bible is the nourisher of our faith, of our devotion and of our understanding of Christ. It is auxiliary to the authority of Christ, not a substitute for it. It is like the photograph of his mother which a young man takes with him into the army. He turns to it again and again to keep vividly before his mind the dear countenance which he cannot now see face to face. But the photograph is not the reality.

The New Testament is a mirror in which is reflected the face of Christ as he was seen by his first disciples and the early church. But the reflection is not the reality. The reality—the real Christ—was alive in the hearts of these first believers, and his living presence has never been withdrawn from his church. It was he, alive in their hearts, who formed them into a community of which he was himself the head. They had no New Testament: they had *him*. The New Testament mirror reflects a many-angled view of him. Its writers did not all see him alike—he was too great for their small hearts, as he is for ours. And the mirror by no means reflects all the divergent views represented by those who, with equal devotion, loved him. But despite their diversity of approach to him, they were one church, which they came to think of as *his body*.

It cannot be too strongly emphasized that the Christian church was in existence and had spread throughout the Roman empire many years before a single book of the New Testament was written. It was born and grew without benefit of the "authority" of the New Testament. Its life was centered in the supreme authority of Jesus Christ. It was their living experience of him that produced the New Testament. The church acknowledged no other allegiance. For every one of its writers, Jesus Christ, the living head of the whole community of believers, held the supreme, undelegated, unshared and indivisible authority.

It is beside the mark to say that the early church had the apostles, that the apostles had the authority and that their authority passed to the New Testament. No apostle, save Paul, wrote any part of the New Testament, so far as we know. And Paul was a convert, not an original disciple who had seen Jesus in the flesh. Moreover, no apostle ever claimed to be an authority in place of Christ. Paul incontinently disclaimed it in his first letter to the Corinthians. And every apostle would have disclaimed it as blasphemy. They called themselves "witnesses," not authorities. They testified to the things they had seen and heard, and to the meaning which they saw in the events which had occurred. In the nature of the case, they would have precedence over all other disciples and would be accorded unique honor in the church. This precedence naturally invested them with the responsibility of leadership in the administration of the church's affairs and the spread of its mission.

The church lived for a hundred years before certain of its scattered writings were collected into an authorized canon, called the New Testament. This was a great event in the history of Christianity. The church was in the way of losing its memory of the events in which Christianity emerged, together with the meaning of the events which the faith of its first-hand witnesses saw in them. Its corporate recollection of these events was of the very genius of Christianity. But the church was invaded by strange philosophies and cults which threatened to obliterate this memory. The collection of the Gospels, the Acts and the Epistles which had meantime been written, became a permanent mirror in which the church could see its own beginnings and so revive and correct its fading memory. Had it not been for this standardization of these classic writings, Christianity might have lost its way in history and become something else than Christianity. The New Testament revitalized the church's corporate memory of Christ and the gospel to which the first disciples had borne witness.

This is the true function of the New Testament, in our time as well as in theirs. It does not rightly take the place of Christ, or of the church's corporate memory of him; it checks and renews this memory as the photograph checks and renews in memory the countenance of a loved one no longer seen in the flesh.

Protestantism and Romanism alike have degraded the Bible

by investing it with a legalistic and literalistic authority equal to or transcending the authority of Christ. The parallel is disconcertingly close. The Protestant misuse of the Bible is essential popery. Like Rome, Protestantism imputes to the writers of the New Testament the status of Christ's "vicegerents on earth"; that is, they were his spokesmen, clothed with his authority; their every word is infallible. Such a status, I repeat, every one of these writers would repudiate as blasphemy, just as Protestants repudiate as blasphemy the claim of the pope to be the successor of one of these apostles. Yet Protestant sectarianism assumes the identical prerogative which the pope assumes in relation to the Bible. We must consider this carefully.

The Roman Church declares the Bible to be the infallible word of God. But the pope declares himself to be its infallible interpreter. The Bible therefore teaches what the pope says it teaches, and he says it teaches that Peter was the "rock" upon which Christ said he would build his church. This authoritarian interpretation of a single text is the basis on which the Roman Church is established. The pope's interpretation thus transcends and supersedes the Bible. No Roman Catholic thinks of looking behind this interpretation to test its validity. That is, it never occurs to him to examine the Bible itself or to inquire of the mind of Christ to see if the pope's interpretation is true.

Protestant sectarianism proceeds in precisely the same manner. The founder of a denomination sets up his particular interpretation of the Bible, or sometimes of a single text of the Bible, as the veritable word of God. Upon this interpretation a denominational "church" is built. The particular interpretation thus becomes a dogmatic stereotype through which his followers read the whole Bible. The stereotype is driven deep into their mentality by constant repetition in the preaching, the teaching and the literature of the group. It gathers support from the sheer fact that it is now embodied in a separate "church." Each such "church" has a distinctive mission. Its mission is to spread its particular interpretation of the Bible. This missionary or evangelistic activity reacts into the interpretation further to crystallize it and to embed the stereotype still more deeply into the collective psychology of the group. Thus the stereotype supersedes the Bible; it carries the authority of the Bible; it *is* the Bible. Anyone who does not see that this is what the Bible says is regarded as either blind or perverse.

All our denominational "churches," from the largest and most respectable to the smallest and more nondescript, are founded and maintain their separate existence on such biblical stereotypes. Each one decrees that its particular interpretation is what the Bible teaches, and it is so certain of the infallibility of its interpretation that it organizes and maintains a "church" —"the true New Testament church"—upon it. This is precisely what Rome does. In both cases, the infallible interpreter cancels out the infallible Bible; the authority of the interpreter cancels out the authority of the Bible; the interpreter becomes the sole authority. Every Protestant denomination is thus, in this fundamental feature, a neat little Roman Catholic church.

Consider how the vast structure of the Roman Church rests upon its particular interpretation of a single text of the Bible, and how thin and insecure its interpretation is. "Thou art Peter" (*petros,* meaning "rock"), Jesus is reported to have said, "and upon this rock [*petra*] I will build my church." It is not necessary to raise here the critical question whether these were indeed the actual words of Jesus or whether they reflect the point of view of a later time when the church was already becoming institutionalized. Yet I must say that the absolute verbal authenticity of the text is open to serious question. But take the statement as it stands. The Roman Church declares that *petra* ("this rock") refers to *petros* (Peter) and that Christ therefore said he would build his church upon Peter. There is no other text in the entire New Testament to corroborate this interpretation, either directly or by implication. Moreover, Peter held no such unique position in the primitive church as would surely be accorded him had he or his fellow apostles known of Jesus' purpose to "build his church" upon him. James, the brother of Jesus, not Peter was the outstanding figure in the Jerusalem church, and Paul once challenged Peter in a crucial matter and held his "authority" in such light esteem that he fearlessly "withstood him to the face."

Protestants have their own interpretation of this text. It is based upon the distinction in gender of *petros* (masculine) and *petra* (feminine). The "rock" upon which Christ declared that he would build his church is held by Protestants to be the *truth* of the good confession that Peter had just made, namely, that Jesus was "the Christ, the Son of the living God." This *petra*, not *petros*, was the "rock" to which Christ referred. Of the two interpretations, I accept the Protestant and incontinently reject the Roman. But speaking for myself alone, I should have to say that if Jesus actually said what the pope says he said in this instance, I would have to deny that Peter spoke the truth when he declared that his Master was the Son of God. A Christ who would build his church on Peter or on any other foundation than himself is not the Lord and Savior I revere. This is a brash but very solemn way of saying that my faith in Christ and my allegiance and devotion to him as the veritable revelation of God do not rest upon the frail basis of any linguistic interpretation of a single text of Scripture.

However, my personal view at this point is not relevant to
the major purpose for which this controversial text is here
introduced. We are concerned with Protestantism. The Roman
Catholic procedure concerns us only because it throws light
on Protestant procedure. The parallel between the Roman
misuse of the Bible as the basis of its "church" and the Protestant misuse of it as the basis of its "churches" is complete.
Both use it to build "churches" upon their particular interpretation of certain selected texts. The sectarian "churches" of
Protestantism are built, as the Roman Catholic Church is
built, upon some text of Scripture—or upon some ingenious
interweaving of selected texts—which becomes a stereotype
through which the whole Bible is thereafter interpreted. This
is perfectly obvious in the marginal sects of Protestantism, such
as those which practice footwashing as a church ordinance
supported by a biblical command, and those which observe
Saturday instead of Sunday. Yet every Protestant sect has its
own "key to the Scriptures," and, like Rome, it builds a
"church" upon the dogma that its favorite scripture supports.

Certainly the practicers of footwashing have a good case.
"Ye ought also to wash one another's feet." There it is, on
the very face of the Bible, and the words are the indisputable words of Jesus himself. There is not even any place for
linguistic hairsplitting here. Likewise, those who practice the
holy kiss as a church ordinance have a good case. "Greet one
another with a holy kiss." This is Paul's plain injunction. You
cannot evade it: it lies open in a definite chapter and verse
of the Scripture. The Protestant ecstatics who work themselves
into a frenzy and "speak with tongues," thinking thereby to
reproduce pentecostal Christianity, have just as good a case
as those more conventional denominations which are built
upon an "ancient order of things" digged with ingenious

skill out of the Acts or the Epistles. The immersionists have
a good case. They first prove to their own satisfaction that
the New Testament word for "baptize" means, in the Greek,
"immerse." Then they hear Christ himself saying, "He that
believeth and is immersed in water shall be saved." And they
hear the apostle saying, "Repent and be immersed in water
every one of you for the remission of your sins." As in the
case of Rome's stereotyped interpretation of its favorite text,
it seems too bad that a divine command with such solemn
consequences should have been left in the ambiguous state
of a debatable linguistic translation. As a matter of fact, the
footwashers and the holy kissers have a better case than the
immersionists or the Roman Catholics, because their favorite
texts are not complicated by the necessity of first establishing
a linguistic point. Their "divine command" is *prima facie*.
There may be, as I believe there are, other grounds upon
which the administration of baptism by immersion can find
plausible support. But the claim that immersion is a biblical
command and therefore a command of Christ and therefore
bound upon his church by his authority and therefore a
sufficient justification for the building of a special "church"
to practice it, is sheer Romanism.

But all these sects, and scores besides, whose "churches"
are "based on the Bible," only follow the pattern set by historical Protestantism, all of whose "churches" have found in
the New Testament "the primitive forms of church order."
These are all stereotypes which have become fixed and established in the mentality of Protestant sectarianism. In the
normal course of denominational activity these stereotypes are,
for the most part, taken for granted in those "churches" that
have attained the status of historical and social respectability.
But in an interdenominational conference of the ecumenical

movement, they take on life and become the subject of endless argument. It does not occur to these denominational protagonists that there is something generically wrong with them all, that their "conscientious convictions" about church order are not derived from Christ, but from a false conception of the Bible or from a reading into the Bible of a stereotype which has been handed down by their denominational tradition.

It is bad enough to degrade the Bible by digging such things out of it, but to degrade and demean Christ by insisting that he has legislated on such matters is hardly short of the unforgivable sin. These representatives of our most respectable and enlightened "churches" show that their thinking proceeds on the same level with that of the footwashers, the holy kissers, the tongue speakers, the immersionists, the Saturday observers, the divine healers and all the rest of the marginal sects whose vagaries and trivialities are not a whit less "scriptural" than their own. And more: they show that their thinking, like that of the rest of Protestant sectarianism, proceeds on the same level as that of Rome, which builds its "church" upon a stereotyped interpretation of a particular biblical text. The only difference is that Rome has a pope to maintain its interpretation, while in Protestant sectarianism the interpretation, once it becomes a stereotype, operates automatically.

One of our larger denominations, at the time of its origin, inscribed on its banner the motto: "Where the Scriptures speak we speak, and where the Scriptures are silent we are silent." This denomination (to which I am honored in belonging) actually imagined, in unwitting arrogance, that it was more loyal, in intention as well as in fact, to the Bible than were Presbyterians, Methodists, Baptists and the rest. Yet all these denominations, with their varying interpretations of the Bible, would affirm with equal solemnity that they, too, speak where the Scriptures speak and are silent where the Scriptures are silent.

Each denomination has historically held its interpretation of the Bible as the standard of loyalty to the Bible itself, and any serious departure from this standard on the part of its members, ministers or churches has been regarded as heresy and visited with the appropriate penalty. Its interpretation was regarded as identical with the Bible—it *was* the Bible. Thus Protestantism has proliferated an astonishing litter of miniature papal infallibilities, each based upon the essential principle in the papacy against which Protestantism had revolted.

Many of our denominations are at last awakening to the absurdity of their historical claim to be uniquely "founded on the Bible." But the delusion still persists in even the most enlightened of them with sufficient vigor to inhibit a full and free recognition of the sole authority of Jesus Christ. And the delusion is resurgent in the fundamentalist movement and other forms of reaction which are disturbing most of the denominations. This resurgence is the penalty which these denominations are paying for their own longtime obsession with the same unscriptural conception of the Bible by which these movements are activated.

The Bible can become the infinitely precious book which Protantism professes it is, only when it is relieved of the incubus of the false authority which Protestant sectarianism has attributed to it. And Christ can come into his exalted place as the Head of his church only when the Bible and every other claimant of authority is subordinated to him.

~ XII ~

THE CONCEPT OF AN
ECUMENICAL PROTESTANTISM

THE BASIS of every Protestant denominational "church," as was demonstrated in the preceding chapter, is the exact duplicate, in principle, of the basis upon which the Roman Catholic Church is founded. It rests upon the substitution of a human authority for the authority of Christ. These denominational "churches" are contradictions of Protestantism within Protestantism. They set up a loyalty to a sectarian interpretation of the Bible which denies their profession of loyalty to the supreme authority of Christ. By dividing his church into "churches," they divide *him,* thus setting Christ against himself.

Whether the essential Protestant principle or the Roman Catholic principle is to prevail in Protestantism is the deepest-cutting issue which Protestantism today confronts. Only as it renounces these remnants of Catholicism which have bedeviled it throughout its history, and sets Christ free from all human "vicegerents"—whether pope, Bible, creed or sectarian "church"—so that he may act with untrammeled authority as the head of his whole church, will Protestantism find its own freedom under Christ to face its responsibility in this age and receive from him the power to discharge it.

The only alternative to a sectarianized Protestantism is an ecumenical Protestantism. By this I mean an ecumenical Protestant church. *Ecumenical*: in the sense that it is inclusive, intentionally and potentially inclusive, though not necessarily at its beginning actually inclusive, of the whole non-Roman Christian community. *Protestant*: in the sense that it rests upon the ecumenical basis of the sovereignty of Christ, and upon no other basis—biblical, creedal or constitutional. A *church*: in the sense of an organic ecclesiastical body, operating with the functions so long usurped by its sectarian "churches"; not a "council" of "churches," nor a "federation" of "churches," nor yet a mere "invisible church," but the actual, empirical, functioning *church of Christ* on earth.

To the exposition of the above paragraph this chapter and the next will be devoted. The paragraph defines a concept—the concept of an ecumenical Protestantism. Whether this concept is realizable, is a question I am not required to answer. It is a question for the Protestant conscience to answer. Protestantism has been intentionally ecumenical from the beginning. It has failed of its intention. Whether it must continue to fail, that is, whether it is incapable of becoming an ecumenical church which shall transcend and annul its present denominational "churches" and embrace in its unity the diversities of its denominations, is the searching question with which the whole ecumenical movement and an America gone secular now confront Protestantism. Its answer will subject the Protestant spirit in every one of its "churches" to a searching test.

It will also—and this is the matter of deepest gravity—test the validity of the Protestant principle of the supreme sovereignty of Christ. It may be—it just may be—that Protestantism, after all, is wrong, and that Christ has to have "on earth"

a "vicar" or a "vicegerent" of some sort to legislate for him
—either a pope or the Bible—together with a motley array of
sects, each one to decree its human interpretation of the Bible
as the infallible truth of the Bible. The consequences of such a
demonstration of the inability of Protestantism to embody its
most basic principle in an ecumenical church are too tragic to
contemplate—tragic for the Christian faith as Protestants have
believed it, and tragic for America which Protestantism will
have definitely lost either to secularism or to Roman Catholicism.

I said above that the question whether the concept of an
ecumenical Protestantism is realizable is for the conscience
of Protestantism to answer. I now add that the Protestant
conscience must also say whether it is willing to be Protestant!
For Protestantism, in its genius and intention, is ecumenical;
in its history and present state, it is not. Protestantism is apostate from itself. It is not ecumenical, because it has proliferated
a multiplicity of "churches" based upon human interpretations
of the Bible and has never brought these interpretations and
these "churches" under the judgment of Christ.

In order to define more clearly the concept of an ecumenical
Protestantism, let us define more clearly its opposite, which
is sectarianism. Sectarianism cannot be defined merely as a
spirit, the spirit of bigotry, though bigotry is likely to be at
the bottom of it and certainly is bred by it. Sectarianism is an
objective ecclesiastical phenomenon, a phenomenon of church
order, and we do not deal with its substantive reality when
we merely deplore, however unctuously, the bigotry which it
breeds. The essence of sectarianism inheres in the fact that
each sect makes itself a "church."

I offer, then, this definition of a sect, as the phenomenon
has been developed in Protestantism: *A sect is a part of the*

ecumenical church of Christ which exercises by itself and for itself those functions which belong to the unity of the ecumenical body of Christ. When these functions are exercised by a part of the church without ecclesiastical responsibility to the whole church, they become schismatic functions and thus define the body which exercises them as a schismatic body or sect. Such all our self-styled "churches" are. The current attempt, following Troeltsch, to distinguish between the "sect type" and the "church type" of denomination has been much overworked. Every Protestant communion or denomination, however "churchly," however long-lived, however respectable, is a sect: it is a self-contained, autonomous ecclesiastical entity arrogating to itself the right to exercise the ecumenical functions of the church of Christ. As the late Archbishop Temple said: "So long as any of us are in schism, all are in schism."

This, the most distinctive feature of our denominations, is entirely overlooked in ecumenical discussions and negotiations. In these discussions a denomination is referred to (1) as a special fellowship within the church of Christ, as indeed it is. Or (2) as the inheritor of a particular tradition, and such it is. Or (3) as composed of like-minded people who hold distinctive convictions about the Bible or the creed or forms of worship or the ministry or the sacraments of baptism and the Lord's Supper. This third conception of the denomination is not so appropriate, perhaps, as it used to be, for every denomination, every sect, from the Protestant Episcopal at one end to the Quakers and Mennonites at the other, includes laity and clergy who represent divergent convictions on all these subjects. But this conception, too, can be passed over without objection, for it, as in the case of (1) and (2), does not really answer the question concerning the nature of a sect.

This question must be answered before the ecumenical movement can deal realistically with its problem.

That question is this: Do those who share such a special fellowship, or such a tradition, or such convictions, have any Christian right to maintain a separate "church" based upon them? By a *Christian* right is meant a right derived from the authority of Christ, a right held and exercised under his approving judgment. The sin and weakness of Protestantism lies in the fact that it has only "churches" but no church. The reason it has no church is not that there is no church, but that its denominational "churches" have usurped the functions by which the true church could make itself known and through which its ecumenical strength could be exercised, under Christ, for the achievement of its divine mission in the world. The goal of the ecumenical aspiration is, therefore, to restore to Protestantism as a united whole the ecumenical functions of which its sectarian "churches" have robbed it.

What are these functions? I shall name eight of them: (1) The ecumenical determination of a general constitution or structural form of the church—its order or polity. (2) The ecumenical function of receiving new members—baptism. (3) The education, selection and appointment of an ecumenical ministry—ordination. (4) The orderly expansion of the ecumenical church into new fields—missions. (5) The inculcation in its membership of the ideals, concepts and lore of the ecumenical Christian faith—Christian education. (6) The ecumenical determination of the general substance and forms of the church's worship—liturgy. (7) The ecumenical administration of the Lord's Supper. (8) A general statement of (a) those beliefs to which the ecumenical church would bear witness before the world, and of (b) the minimum but central belief which it would require for admission into its membership. These two statements, presumably, would not be identical.

All these are ecclesiastical functions which can be exercised only by a corporate organic body. The goal of Christian unity is nothing less than the attainment of an ecumenical church within which all these functions are exercised by the whole church for the church as a whole. Each is a true function of the ecumenical church of Christ. But every one of them is now exercised by the denominational "churches" (sects), within a self-enclosed ecclesiastical autonomy the effect of whose action extends only to the borders of the denomination. That is, no denominational "church" can presume to perform these functions for the whole church and on behalf of the whole church. It is true that some denominations do recognize the validity of the acts of other denominations in the performance of these functions. But this is an expression of Christian fellowship and comity; it is not implicit in the performance of the act. Those denominations, such as the Baptists and Disciples, which do not recognize the validity of the baptism administered by other denominations, and insist upon rebaptism, are thoroughly consistent with the logic of sectarianism, though all other Christians (and, happily, an increasing number of Baptists and Disciples) hold that such a practice is unecumenical and grossly un-Christian.

The concept of an ecumenical Protestantism can become a living reality only by the surrender of the functions of "churchly" sovereignty, now exercised by its denominations, to the ecumenical church of Christ itself. This means that its denominations must cease to be "churches." But even if they should desire, in loyalty to Christ, to cease being "churches" and to surrender their sovereignty, they would be faced with a dilemma. There exists no ecumenical Protestantism to which the surrender of their "churchly" sovereignty could be made.

How are these "churches" to bring such an ecumenical church into existence?

Three procedures are open: (1) cooperation on a federal basis, (2) progressive reduction of the number of denominations by mergers, (3) a concerted upsurge of the Protestant conscience demanding an ecumenical church now. The first two are already in operation. The third is only beginning to find overt expression, but it is cherished as a hope and a prayer in the hearts of innumerable Christians of all denominations. Let us examine these three open ways to an ecumenical Protestantism with a view to measuring how far we have already gone and how far we have yet to go.

1. *Cooperation on a federal basis.* Some twenty-five denominations have been working together in a federal cooperation for more than a generation—long enough to have developed a spirit of mutual trust, a sense of the inner unity of Protestantism, and a strong purpose to widen the scope of their common aims as these aims emerge in consciousness under the pressure of events and the experience of fellowship. I refer, of course, to the Federal Council of the Churches of Christ in America, whose constituent denominations are banded together "for the prosecution of work that can be better done in union than in separation."

A generation ago, when this organization was launched, the number of things that the denominations were willing to "do in union" was cautiously limited. And it is still limited, but the number has substantially increased through the years. The council's original functions also have been appreciably expanded. Most of its functions, however, lie in a domain outside of the ecclesiastical order. This is its limitation. The denominations still retain all the eight above mentioned ecclesiastical functions in their separate and sovereign control. The Federal

Council has not been invested with any prerogative relating to the internal affairs of its constituent "churches." It can act for them only as each of them gives its consent to specific cooperative measures. But as they work together outside the ecclesiastical domain—on questions of public policy, world peace, race relations, evangelism, industrial relations, the protection of the family, and numerous other matters not involving questions of church order or doctrine—it is becoming clear that certain other functions long exercised by the independent sovereignty of the sectarian "churches" are among those things "that can be better done in union than in separation."

A slight but significant advance into the ecclesiastical jurisdiction of the denominational "churches" is the adoption of a code of comity, under which the "churches" agree to behave with some decent measure of respect for one another in the extension of their denominations into new fields. The acceptance of such a limitation upon an ecclesiastical prerogative which the denominational "churches" have always exercised without the slightest regard for one another is an action in the interest of ecumenical Protestantism. It suggests the practicability of applying the federal principle still further within the ecclesiastical domain.

The Federal Council can be conceived as the medium in which this growth of an ecumenical Protestantism can take place in a parallel development with the growth of the ecumenical conscience itself. It requires only that the principle of doing together those things "that can be better done in union than in separation" be applied, not only in the extra-ecclesiastical domain, as now, but in the ecclesiastical domain as well. In addition to the code of comity above referred to, a considerable degree of cooperation has already been attained, outside the Federal Council, in the administration of two of the eight ecclesiastical functions which I have listed above as ecumenical. These are (1) the missionary enterprise and (2) religious education, each of them being a true function of the ecumenical church, but long administered by the denominational "churches." True, such cooperation as now exists in these fields is only partially and passively recognized by the denominations. It has grown up among their boards or other agencies which are still under denominational control. But it it real and substantial, and points in the direction of a more basic and conscious integration.

In the Foreign Missions Conference and the Home Missions Council nearly all the boards of the denominations are now cooperatively administering the missionary enterprise. In the International Council of Religious Education the denominations carry on a large part of the function of religious education cooperatively. In neither of these fields, however, do these organizations presume to act ecumenically. The ultimate administration of both functions is still retained by the denominations, which continue to exercise their autonomous ecclesiastical prerogatives. But the step from such cooperation to an ecumenical administration of the whole missionary and the whole educational function is short. It could be accomplished by the union of these organizations with the Federal Council, and the deliberate transference of the sectarian prerogatives by which they are now administered denominationally to the inclusive organization.

There will be some timid ecclesiastics who will shrink from the exposition of these possibilities. Their thesis will be that it is better to continue to let the Federal Council and these other agencies of cooperation be thought of as static, having no significance beyond their present modes of functioning.

church, under Christ, can do this, and, in our time, that means only an ecumenical church. It is high time that the first step in the evolution of such an ecumenical Protestantism were taken.

I do not say that the transfer of the missionary and educational functions to the Federal Council (or to its successor resulting from a union with the two other agencies), to be administered ecumenically, would transform that agency into a church. Far from it! Protestantism would still have much to do before a true ecumenical church could emerge.

What I do say is that the Federal Council and the two missions conferences and the council on religious education, having already established the principle of cooperation up to a certain point, are now in a providential position, by uniting in one agency, to enlist the denominations in *an ecumenical administration* of these two ecumenical functions and so awaken the first gleams of a genuine ecumenical consciousness throughout Protestantism. This nascent consciousness, under the kindling influence of the Spirit of God, will point the separated "churches" *in the direction of an ecumenical Protestant church*. It will open the way for the transfer of other ecumenical functions to the federal body.

The reflex influence upon the "churches" which have once committed their sectarian missionary and educational functions to a common administration will naturally prompt them to explore other possibilities in the same direction. They would naturally ask, Why should not the training of the Christian ministry be undertaken ecumenically instead of denominationally? No good reason could be given for the continuance of sectarian theological schools. The reason for their existence is steadily diminishing with the decline of the sectarian spirit and the emergence of an ecumenical theology. The united administration of missions and Christian education would plainly call for the training of an ecumenically minded ministry.

It is not too much to say that the denominational seminaries have been the mainstay of sectarianism. In producing ministers whose minds have been molded under the illusion that their denominational tradition is, if not the whole of Christianity, at least the central core and substance of it, the leadership of the "churches" is committed in advance to the psychology of sectarianism. The denomination and its interests intensively preoccupy the mind of such a ministry, and the ecumenical church is recognized as hardly more than a marginal interest to which it pays only an occasional gesture of respect. Not until the ecumenical aspiration is embodied in the schools where the Christian ministry is being trained will this inversion of values be corrected. It will not be corrected so long as each denomination insists upon the training of its ministers in sectarian isolation.

The training of an ecumenically minded ministry must go hand in hand with the emergence of an ecumenical church. When the denominations, cooperating under the federal principle, have once committed their missionary and educational functions to a unitary administration, supported by the denominations but no longer administered by them, it may be expected that the function of training ministers in detached seminaries under denominational control will be seen as an anachronism, obstructive of the emerging ecumenical unity.

As a matter of present fact the seminaries themselves are becoming aware of the irrational basis upon which their separatism rests. The differences between their teaching are matched by the same differences within the faculty of each particular seminary. Instead of continuing to foster the illusion that each seminary has some peculiar body of instruction for which the denomination requires a seminary of its own, it is high time for each denomination to recognize that whatever "distinctive truth" it may imagine that it possesses can be imparted in a free ecumenical seminary with promise of a far wider acceptance than in the exclusiveness of a sectarian institution.

I have no intention of following further this line of possible development under the federal principle. But it must now be plain that when once the ecumenical functions of Christian missions, Christian education and the training of the Christian ministry—all now administered denominationally—have been transferred to a common administration, a nascent ecumenical entity will have emerged, the nucleus of the true church of Christ, an entity having both substance and form, both spirit and body, comprehending and, so far forth, uniting the whole of participating Protestantism. With the achievement of such a degree of unity on the level of practical functioning, it is not difficult to imagine that the more interior, sectarian barriers to unity—polity, creed, baptism, the eucharist, ordination—would melt away and the full-orbed ecumenical church come into empirical existence. The federal principle, having served as a means to this great consummation, would disappear as applied to a sectarian order that would no longer exist. But it could continue to serve as the vital link between geographical or regional units (dioceses, synods, jurisdictions—whatever the nomenclature) of the united church.

2. *The reduction of the number of denominations by mergers.* This process has been under way for some time. Notable instances in which two or more denominational "churches" have united to form one "church" mark a signal

development of the ecumenical spirit. Since 1906, fourteen such mergers have taken place. Others are now in process of negotiation. These mergers may be conceived as way stations on the road to an ecumenical Protestantism. They represent, negatively, a loosening of sectarian bonds which inevitably accompanies a sincere response to the ecumenical spirit. And they represent, positively, the longing of Christian people for a church more worthy of their allegiance than the sectarian fragment of the church whose weakness and irrelevance are increasingly apparent. These mergers, however, fall short of satisfying this longing. The new "church" formed by the union of two or more denominations is still a fragment of the church of Christ. The dislocations in familiar procedures require new adjustments, and the assimilation of hitherto separated fellowships into one fellowship may require much patience and grace. Whether the goal achieved is sufficiently commanding to inspire the united body with the required patience and grace will depend upon the degree in which the merger is recognized as only a way station on the road to a comprehensive ecumenical church. If the merger is so conceived, the adjustment of difficulties will seem a small price to pay for the temporary dilution of denominational morale by the unfamiliarities which the merger necessarily brings with it. If the merger, on the other hand, is conceived as virtually an end in itself, without conscious dedication to the ultimate goal, the unfamiliarites of adjustment in procedures and in fellowship may cause the larger "church" to be even less efficient than its constituent denominations were before their union.

As a rule, these mergers are negotiated and achieved principally on the basis of their sectarian agreements; and these sectarian features tend to persist in the consciousness of the new "church" in much the same manner as they existed in the units prior to the merger. Even this, however, is a positive gain whose importance cannot be discounted. But it is not necessarily an advance toward an ecumenical Protestantism. It will mark such an advance only if its basis of union is ecumenical in principle and intention, and if the new "church" is informed with the ecumenical spirit. Such a "church" would then be spiritually potent as a participant in the movement toward an ultimate ecumenical Protestantism, and in any steps leading to that goal. But if the merger is based merely upon the happy fact that the units are already in agreement on the sectarian features which both share, the result will be only the reduction of the number of denominations, and the achievement, so far as its ecumenical significance is concerned, will be virtually static.

In this general movement for the merger of denominations, what is now needed is the demonstration of the ecumenical principle by the merger of certain denominations whose sectarian features and traditions are *unlike*. This would constitute an unambiguous advance toward the ecumenical goal, because it would provide an example and a pattern for a similar union of multiple "churches" on a larger scale. For this reason, the negotiations between "churches" representing separate ecclesiastical traditions, such as the Congregational Christian with the Evangelical and Reformed, on the one hand, and the Episcopal with the Presbyterian, on the other, both now under way, carry great promise and are being watched with prayerful hope.

THE CONCEPT OF AN
ECUMENICAL PROTESTANTISM
(Continued)

WE HAVE BEEN discussing how an ecumenical Protestantism can be achieved. Our outlook is limited to America, which sectarian Protestantism has been progressively losing for three generations and which only an ecumenical Protestantism can hope to win. Two possibilities have been envisaged. One, the gradual development of an organically united church through the progressive broadening of the federal principle to apply to the ecclesiastical as well as the extra-ecclesiastical functions of the denominations. The other, merging of denominations by twos or threes, thus building up stronger denominations and at the same time illustrating the possibility of a more general and inclusive rapprochement. Both these procedures represent the attainment of the goal by a process of gradualism.

We have now to consider a possibility which, even to envisage it, will call for a more daring imagination, a more prophet-like courage, a more sensitive response to the urgency of the hour and a profounder faith in the readiness of the Christian conscience to yield to the will of God.

3. *A concerted upsurge of the Protestant conscience de-*

manding an ecumenical church now. Promising as are the
approaches by federalism and mergers, they require time; and
the question the "churches" must face is whether there is time
enough! Protestantism is not winning America now, and it
will not win it by the federation of denominations so long
as they continue to function as separate and independent
"churches," nor by the progressive merging of these "churches"
into larger but still separate "church" units. Only an ecumenical Protestantism can match the formidable magnitudes
which the Christian faith confronts in our day. Only an ecumenical Protestantism can command the devotion and evoke
the allegiance of individual Christians and local churches
which the task of winning America to Christ requires. This
devotion and this allegiance are disappearing with the increasing irrelevance of every Protestant denomination. The
dynamic of the Christian faith cannot be recaptured by any
scheme or contrivance which embraces or tolerates the
"churchly" pretensions of these denominations. Only the
church of Christ itself is worthy to receive the devotion or
able to release the dynamic which Protestantism must have if
it is to arrest its own decay.

The evolutionary process of federalism and mergers might
be trusted to lead to this goal—if there were time. But is there
time? May not the process of Protestant decay continue *pari
passu* with the slow development of federalism and the piece-
meal procedure of attaining unity by mergers? Will secularism
wait upon this super-cautious, timid and slow advance of
Protestantism toward an ecumenical unity? Will Roman Catholicism wait? Will the innumerable cults and fanaticisms
that are boring into Protestantism, dividing it still further and
draining off its members—will these wait?

Can the Protestant conscience itself wait? Is not Protestantism already sufficiently disquieted by the impotence, the effrontery and the irrelevance of its sectarianism to be willing to do something about it—to do something now, to cut the red tape of all schemes of gradualism and, by taking direct action, stand forth in its true ecumenical character? I believe that Protestantism, over a large section of its "churches," is more ready to act than its ecclesiastical leaders realize. If these leaders, instead of solemnly urging caution and thus quenching the struggling flame of ecumenical fellowship, would release the inhibitions which come from their own professional implication in the denominational system, and let the Spirit of Christ have its way, it is not too difficult to believe that there would be a concerted upsurge of the Protestant conscience demanding an ecumenical Protestantism.

Optimistic reflection in this vein has been reinforced by a recent action taken by the Federal Council of Churches inviting those denominations which "recognize one another's ministries and sacraments" to send delegates to a conference to explore the possibilities of closer union. This action was prompted by overtures addressed to the Federal Council by two denominations asking it to call such a conference. The response of the "churches," at this writing, is only beginning to be made.

The possibilities inherent in such a conference kindle the imagination. Many denominations, at the grass roots of their consciousness, are already convicted of the sinful irrelevance of their sectarian "churchism" and would be ready to surrender their illegitimate functions to an ecumenical church which would then and there emerge. This would be an event in the history of Christianity more significant than any that has occurred since the Reformation. Should a substantial number of these denominational "churches" find themselves "with one accord in one place"—a sufficient number to give "body" to their concerted action—it would be a veritable Pentecost on a grand scale. The church that would then and there emerge might not be ecumenical in the sense of all-inclusive, but it would be such in principle and intention, for it would throw its doors wide open for all other Protestant "churches" to enter. It would follow the lead of the United Church of Canada, whose motto is: "Not only a united church, but a uniting church."

Let us assume that the movement to attain an ecumenical Protestantism is crowned with success, whether by evolution under the federal principle or by mergers of denominations or by a spontaneous pentecostal response to the Spirit of Christ. What, it will be asked, will then become of the denominations? The answer is simple: they can live just as long as they want to live! There will be room for them all in an ecumenical church, for that is of the genius of such a church. There is no wrong, no sin, in being a denomination. The sin is in erecting the denomination into a "church." It is the "church-ism" of the denominations that divides Christ's body. This is the point at which our denominational system becomes sin —it is sin because it denies to the ecumenical church, which is the only true church, the possibility of coming into empirical existence.

There are little denominations, so to speak, within all our denominational "churches," and there will always be denominations inside of the ecumenical church. Our present denominations may continue to exist in an ecumenical Protestantism so long as there is life and reality in their tradition. Many of them, I imagine, would soon disappear because, shorn of their "churchly" pretensions, there would be little vitality left. The reasons for their existence have long since become obsolete. But new groupings would be continually appearing. By this I mean to say that there will always be diversity of opinion, of creed, of practice, of taste, of fellowship affinities in the church of Christ. Such diversities are not evil; they are good; they are the conditions of growth, and contribute to the spiritual and theological enrichment of the whole church. The sin of sectarianism is that these diversities have been used to multiply "churches" based upon them, under the illusion that, by walling off their peculiar diversity within a separate and exclusive "church," the particular tenet of such a "church" could be both cherished and propagated.

This is not only an illusion, but the most tragic delusion of which Protestantism has been the victim. The history of sectarianism clearly shows that the original tenet upon which a "church" was founded tends to become hollow, unreal and static even to its own members; and this often occurs within two generations or less. Moreover, the notion that any divergent creed or practice or polity requires that a separate "church" be created in order to propagate it, is disproved by the whole history of sectarianism. The effect is just the contrary. It tends to put that tenet out of circulation. If the tenet is true, or the practice or polity is sound, it would fare better were it maintained on its merits, with Christian consideration, within the fellowship of the ecumenical church. But once it is sectarianized in an autonomous "church," it raises barriers of prejudice and pride against its acceptance. There is no surer guarantee that its truth will not be accepted beyond its own walled-in sect than to crystallize and isolate it in the form of a separate "church."

Furthermore, every denominational "church" tends to exaggerate its tenets out of all proportion to their merits or their importance and to blind itself to the merits of the position held by others. A sectarian "church" not only shuts its own faithful in, and others equally faithful out; it also shuts its own truth in, and other truth out. Its own truth cannot get out to win its way on its merits; and the truth held by others cannot get in to correct its errors and enrich its thought. But the Christian faith and the democratic principle alike require a free circulation of truth and error. Sectarianism isolates truth and coddles error. This point requires a somewhat extended consideration before I can bring this already long exposition to a close.

It is illustrated in matters not only of creed, but also of church polity. Every denominational "church" tends to exaggerate out of all proportion the distinctiveness and the merit of its own type of organization. As a matter of fact, there is no vital difference between the various systems represented by the Episcopal, the Methodist, the Presbyterian, the Lutheran and others in the same general category. And the differences between these "churches" and the congregationally organized "churches"—Baptists, Disciples and Congregationalists—which erroneously imagine that they are more "democratic" because they are less organic!—is by no means so great in practice as in abstract theory. But the differences among them all are exaggerated far beyond reality by a psychological process which goes on in the ecclesiastical isolation of their separated "churches." This process could be described as *the inbreeding of the illusion of distinctiveness.*

The effect of this inbreeding process is to produce a particular type of mentality which characterizes every one of the denominations. I cannot find a word which better describes it than to call it a "huddling" mentality. It is a state of mind that is generated by huddling in the self-enclosed sectarian groups, isolated from the open forum of ecumenical Christianity. Huddling is the favorite indoor sport of every denomination. Inside the sectarian enclosure, the victims of this mentality keep endlessly churning over and over the notions which belong to the "tradition" of that particular huddle. These notions are thus magnified into an importance which cannot bear the light of the out-of-doors, the open arena or forum where they have to meet on a broad front the realities of life. This mentality is not limited to small minds only; it infects the greatest men in our denominations. Men of otherwise large intellectual caliber become positively hypnotized with a sectarian fixation. Illustrations abound.

I could select an example from my own denomination. But I choose rather to give a typical illustration that lies at hand in the form of an extended statement on Christian unity which a distinguished Episcopal bishop recently addressed to his diocese. The statement was obviously prompted by the then current negotiations between Episcopalians and Presbyterians with respect to the possibility of their union. The bishop uses the most unqualified language (with which the language I have used in these pages cannot vie) in his presentation of the need of a united church. Give heed to his vigorous words:

In this great day of need and opportunity, the Christian church stands with its witness weakened and its message confused and obscured by its own differences and divisions. A church that is divided and disunited cannot preach Christ with full power. Only a united Christian church can effectively call this world to that belief in the absolute sovereignty of God and in the universal supremacy of his moral law, which is the world's only hope.

After the bishop's elaboration of this theme at great length, one would expect some warm recognition of the Presbyterian Church, if not of Protestant "churches" in general, as a part of the ecumenical church of Christ. And as the inevitable corollary of this recognition, one would expect an expression of the imperative duty to find a way to end the scandal of their separation. But no, the good bishop retreated into his sectarian huddle and proceeded to extol "the three great, central principles, the Apostolic Faith, the Apostolic Sacraments, and the Apostolic Ministry of Bishops, Priests and Deacons" (the bishop's capitalization) which, he alleged, the Episcopal Church represents, and which, by implication, the Presbyterian and other Protestant "churches" do not represent. In holding these "three great principles," the Episcopal Church, the bishop maintained, is not Protestant; yet it is not Roman Catholic. It occupies the position of a "bridge" between Roman Catholicism and Protestantism.

We have here a perfect example of the huddling psychology of sectarianism which results from the inbreeding of the illusion of distinctiveness. The good bishop is totally unaware of the blind inconsistency of his remarks, as every sectarian pleader is. In one breath he deplores division, and in the next claims that his own "church" is a "bridge" between those who have the apostolic faith, the apostolic sacraments and the apostolic ministry and those who have them not! His "bridge church," however, has them all. Let the reader keep in mind just what these three things are. They are not minor or marginal matters—they are the structural essentials of any church that can claim to be Christian. Yet the bishop, by implication, denies that the Presbyterian and other Protestant "churches" possess these essentials. Why, then, is division so deplorable? And why is union desirable or even thinkable with "churches" that do not have the apostolic faith, the apostolic sacraments and the apostolic ministry?

The bishop is only indulging in the favorite indoor sport of denominationalism. His out-of-doors mind is expressed in his strong words deploring division and pleading for unity, a unity which, one would suppose, is neither possible nor desirable with those who do not have the apostolic faith, the apostolic sacraments and the apostolic ministry. His indoor mind is expressed in his implied denial that other Protestant "churches" possess the apostolic faith, the apostolic sacraments and the apostolic ministry. The inconsistency is covered up for him by the concept of the "bridge church." This concept has been nursed and fondled so long in the Episcopal huddle that it has become a refuge for the inaction into which a considerable section of that "church" automatically retreats after the most unctuous and even grandiose asseverations of the imperative need of a united church. The concept invites examination.

What is the function of a bridge? It is something that enables one to cross over from one side of a cleft to the other. Upon such a bridge the Episcopal Church takes its stand. Who is going to cross over? Is the Roman Church going to cross over to the Protestant side? It is welcome, everlastingly welcome, to come; but it will not be the Roman Church when it comes; it will be Protestant. Will the Episcopal Church join Rome in coming over? Or will it remain on the bridge? If it intends to join Rome in coming over to the Protestant side, why not come now?

Or, is Protestantism expected to cross over to the Roman side? If it does, it will be no longer Protestant, but Roman Catholic. And if it does, will the Episcopal Church join Protestantism in going to Rome, or will it remain on the bridge? Of course, a movement in either of these directions is inconceivable. Neither the Roman Church nor Protestantism is going to cross over. They are absolutely irreconcilable.

What, then, is in the good bishop's mind when he expatiates on the unique position which the Episcopal Church occupies on the "bridge"? Can it be anything else than an appeal to both Protestantism and Catholicism to meet *on the bridge itself?* That is, to find their unity by absorption in the Episcopal Church! I can find no other meaning in the bishop's words, and I doubt that he or those Episcopalians who hold this view can otherwise explain the "bridge" concept. I do not believe that this venerable prelate represents the serious out-of-doors thinking of the Episcopal communion. The "bridge" concept is a mere psychological contrivance devised by the sectarian spirit to keep the Episcopal Church itself from having to decide whether it will leave its "bridge" and go definitely to one side or the other.

The time has come, as Reinhold Niebuhr has recently said, for the Anglican communion "to make a decision on the meaning of the Reformation." "It must decide," he says, "whether it regards the Reformation, on the whole, as an aberration or a creative event in the history of the Christian faith, an event which delivered the church from the heresy of identifying itself with the Kingdom of God and of making a particular and highly authoritarian organization of the church the only possible basis for a world-wide Christian fellowship."

Surely, the evangelical and truly Protestant voices in the Episcopal communion will speak with more vigor as the crisis of such an inescapable decision approaches. Episcopalianism has much to give to the rest of Protestantism and nothing at all to give to Rome. It is inconceivable that the Anglican communion will ever cross to the Roman side. Its catholic elements are not Roman Catholic. They are potentially Protestant. An ecumenical Protestantism would include them—

filtered, no doubt, as the elements in all the denominations would be filtered, in the process of becoming ecumenical. By renouncing the empty and illusory concept of a "bridge" over an impassable chasm and orienting itself definitely within the Protestant Reformation, the sincerity of Episcopal protestations on behalf of Christian unity would be cleared of all ambiguity.

This illustration of sectarian psychology which has been selected from the Episcopal Church is duplicated in varying degrees in the psychology of all the denominations. My own is no less the victim of this indoor inbreeding of sectarian illusions than any other. Indeed, the Disciples of Christ could provide an almost perfect parallel to the "bridge" delusion. But I shall not expose it! What little courage I could summon up to speak plainly to my Episcopal brethren has been exhausted. And prudence suggests the unwisdom of jeopardizing the peaceable relations which I enjoy with my own denominational family!

The moral to be drawn from this discussion is obvious. The concept of an ecumenical Protestantism requires a profound searching of heart on the part of every denominational leader to see "if there be any wicked way" of sectarianism in him. If he is honest with his own soul, he will surely find something there of which to repent. There can be no advance toward this high goal save as there is a spiritual revolution in the mind and conscience of the whole Protestant community, from the ecclesiastic upon whom rests the responsibility of general direction to the parish ministers and the laity of their churches. By a spiritual revolution is meant the emancipation of the mind of Protestantism from the fixations and complexes which have been generated in sectarian isolation; the utter abandonment of the delusion that the things which separate the denominations are so important and crucial as to require or justify their continued existence as "churches"; the utter abandonment of the delusion that Protestantism, operating in the medium of its system of denominational "churches," can win America to Christ.

Such an inward spiritual change of heart will inhibit any further pious trifling with the concept of ecumenical Protestantism. Long enough have Protestant leaders played with the idea, announcing it and even advocating it, only to nullify it by adding an interpolated weasel sentence designed not only to mollify the sectarian spirit but to inhibit action. The slogan: "Not church union, but Christian unity," is typical of such weasel words. The antithesis is false. Christian unity we already have: all Christians are already one—united in Christ who is the living head of us all.

The issue does not lie in that spiritual dimension. It lies in the ecclesiastical dimension. The ecumenical problem is an ecclesiastical problem, and must be faced squarely as such. The issue can be stated thus: Shall American Protestantism let Christ be the head of *his church?* This question indicates the crisis to which Protestantism has been brought by the relative deterioration of its strength in American society on the one hand, and the emerging foregleams of an ecumenical conscience on the other.

~ XIV ~

PROTESTANTISM AND THE
LORDSHIP OF CHRIST

AS PROTESTANTISM becomes conscious of the magnitude of its task, it needs to be set free to mobilize its forces in a manner adequate to match it. Only a strong Protestantism can hope to penetrate the strongly entrenched citadels of secularism and to match the aggressive advance of a highly integrated and powerful Catholicism. But so long as Protestantism is held down, and held apart, by the sectarian obsession that its organization must meticulously conform to an ancient order, so long will it fail to assume its high responsibility to win America. Christ himself has made the intelligence of his church forever free from any such bondage.

In the assumption of this responsibility and in the consciousness of its freedom, there is one paramount consideration by which the course of American Protestantism must be determined. This is an unqualified and undivided loyalty to Jesus Christ. This perhaps should go without saying. But it desperately needs to be said, for it carries far-reaching implications. There are, of course, lesser loyalties which this supreme loyalty subtends—loyalty to the Bible, to one's creedal beliefs, to a denominational tradition, to Protestantism

176

itself. All such loyalties must, however, be held subordinate to Christ, constantly re-examined in his presence, under his judgment, to make sure that they are not superseding him, that is, being used as his "vicegerents." No one of them can be allowed to subtend *him*.

To say this is to affirm the whole substance of Protestantism. Despite its obscuration of Christ's supreme authority by its misuse of the Bible, its divisive use of creeds and its fissiparous creation of a multitude of "churches" based upon human authority, Protestantism has affirmed, from the beginning to this day, however inconsistently, the absolute headship and Lordship of Christ in his church. Its weakness and shame inhere in the fact that it has given these lesser loyalties priority over loyalty to him, thus using him to sanction them. His sovereignty has been made pendent to *them*, as it is in Roman Catholicism.

The supreme imperative that now rests upon Protestantism is to release the immanent, undelegated and indivisible sovereignty of Christ from the incubus under which self-constituted human authorities, that is, sectarian "churches," have smothered it. In responding to this imperative, the all-important thing is to begin at the right place. If we begin at the wrong place, the difficulties will be exaggerated and multiplied. The wrong place to begin is in the realm of the lesser loyalties—the Bible, the creed, the sacraments, church order. The ecumenical movement, to which I am deeply devoted, has, I am bound to say, begun at the wrong place. It has concerned itself with the lesser loyalties before coming to terms with the supreme loyalty. These subordinate and relative loyalties rightly belong to the Christian faith, and their consideration at the right time and in the right context is not only proper but irrepressible. But the context and framework in which they can be rightly considered must be determined by the authority of Christ.

The presupposition behind the present procedure of the ecumenical movement is that agreement must be reached in respect to these theological and ecclesiological matters before an ecumenical church under the sovereignty of Christ is possible. Such a procedure is foredoomed; for, even if an "ecumenical" church were achieved on the basis of agreement in this realm, it would carry within itself no principle of permanency. It would surely be upset by the emergence of new disagreements. Let it be written down as an indisputable premise of any true ecumenical procedure that there will always be conceptual diversity and disagreement in the Christian community in the realm of the lesser loyalties. Such diversities are to be welcomed, not deplored. They are signs of life; their absence would be a sign of stagnation and decadence.

If there is to be an ecumenical church at all, it must rest upon a basis that provides a welcome for these diversities and embraces them. The hope of uniformity on the plane of these lesser loyalties is fatuous. An ecumenical church can rest only upon the church's supreme loyalty. It must rest upon the Lordship of Christ, and upon this alone. *His sovereign authority is the only ecumenical principle in Christianity.* Everything else—I say it sweepingly—*everything else*—Bible, creed, sacraments, tradition, "ancient order of things"—is divisive, sectarian, hopeless, when it is held without being referred to Christ for his judgment upon it. When so held it tends inevitably to divide the church instead of uniting it. In seeking unity on these matters as a prerequisite to an ecumenical church, the ecumenical movement is following the lead of Roman Catholicism and denying the essential genius of Protestantism, just as every sectarian "church" in Protestantism denies it.

The true starting point in dealing with our differences in this realm of the lesser loyalties is to bring them all under the judgment of Christ, to see them as he sees them, to appraise their importance as he appraises it, and to give them the place in his church which he determines. Only as we know his mind can we have any criterion by which to determine our ecclesiastical behavior in respect to our denominational differences.

Is it possible, then, to know the mind of Christ on those matters which divide his church? It is not only possible, but all Protestants confess that they already know it. His judgment in this realm is not in controversy. There are other realms in which Christians differ as to what the mind of Christ requires—the ethical realm, for example. Radical differences appear in the application of Christ's teaching to concrete problems of moral conduct. Christians are not agreed on what the mind of Christ requires of his followers with respect to participation in war, or even with respect to their participation in government. The whole field of the political and economic organization of society presents problems on which Christians make opposing interpretations of the mind of Christ. Certain aspects of the family, notably the matter of divorce and remarriage, cause sharp disagreement among those who devoutly seek to know what Christ would have his followers do. In these and many other departments of human living the mind of Christ is in controversy.

But in the realm of the constitution of his church there is no controversy among Protestants. The unanimous voice of the Protestant conscience proclaims that the only church Christ recognizes as his is the ecumenical church. The living church of which Christ is the living head transcends all denominational "churches" and includes the whole community of those who acknowledge his Lordship.

Every Protestant denomination will affirm this. No denomination claims that Christ is the head of its denomination! It may claim that it has "the truth," that it is "the true New Testament church," that its creed is the true statement of the Christian faith, and that its practices and mode of organization conform strictly to the "pattern" of the primitive church; but no denomination, or only a negligible few, has ever pretended that Christ is the head of its denomination. Such a claim would sound either ridiculous or blasphemous in the ear of any Protestant. Only Rome makes such a claim, and it was against this very pretension that Protestantism revolted.

Protestantism thus knows at least this much of the mind of Christ with respect to the differences which divide his church into "churches": He totally disregards them as having no relevancy at all in the constitution of his church. Protestants confess that Christ and his church transcend their sectarian contentions and the sectarian "churches" that are maintained upon them. The sheep of other sectarian folds belong to him no less than those of their own sectarian fold. They belong to him, not alone because they all claim him, but because he recognizes and actually receives all of them as his own.

Yet every sectarian "church," by its very existence as such a "church," denies the truth that its conscience affirms. By virtue of being what it is—that is, a *church*—it denies that Christ has received others as he has received those of its sectarian fellowship. It maintains a separate, full-panoplied ecclesiastical "church," which arrogates to itself the right to exercise for itself all the functions that belong to the ecumenical church. Every denominational "church" is thus a contradiction and denial of Protestantism. Here is the crux of the issue between a sectarian Protestantism and an ecumenical Protestantism. It does not lie in any controversial realm; it is an issue in the realm of the Protestant conscience.

Note carefully what all this implies as to the Lordship and authority of Christ: If he has received us all—Presbyterians, Episcopalians, Methodists, Congregationalists, Baptists, Disciples, Lutherans and all the rest—if we all belong to *his* church, it clearly follows that *he* holds the things that divide us as unworthy of the importance with which we have invested them. We stand condemned under his judgment for doing violence to his church and dividing *him* by maintaining sectarian "churches" of our own making. His church is not sufficient for us, and so we make a kind of "church" that suits *us*. We thus demean his Lordship, affront his authority, and cripple his divine mission. Every one of these "churches" is based upon egotistic, humanistic conceptions and purposes which, in his eyes, have no place in the constitution of his church.

The Protestant conscience thus confesses that the lesser loyalties on which every sectarian "church" is based are purely human ideologies and pragmatic functions concerning which the authority of Christ has left his church free. They do not belong, in any sense, to the *constitution* of the church; they belong in the area of its *fellowship*. The differences among those who acknowledge Christ as divine Lord and Savior and who seek to know his will that they may obey it, are real differences and cannot be suppressed. But there is not a single issue in the whole controversial realm that rightly belongs to the constitution of the church. To build a "church" upon it is to deny the Lordship of Christ which embraces the members of other "churches" in his church. All these differences are differences *among Christians,* among those whom

Christ has himself received into his church. *His* church therefore embraces these differences, transcends them and makes a place within itself for their consideration. The fellowship of the ecumenical church transcends all ethical, doctrinal and organizational differences. And only the ecumenical church is the church of Christ. It is in the spiritual democracy of this fellowship—in the free and open exchange of convictions, accompanied by the Christian spirit of forbearance and mutual deference, that these diversities of conviction may be maintained for what they are, namely, human opinions and pragmatic procedures. In that fellowship, which sees all such differences as Christ sees them and refrains from investing them with an importance above that in which he holds them, they may be maintained, reconciled, or forgotten.

To one whose mind has been molded by our Protestant sectarianism this will seem like a fantastic picture. "Do you mean to say," he will ask, "that the Lordship of Christ is a sufficient principle for the constitution of the ecumenical church?" Yes, that is what I have pointedly affirmed. "But," he will continue, "human nature will not stand for it! You cannot expect people who hold such diversities of conviction to live together in one church! Inevitably they will separate into 'churches' of their own making." Perhaps that is true, and it is well to have the objection stated so plainly. If our sectarian "churches," set up to embody some human interpretation of the Bible or some creed or some particular form of church order, are an expression of "human nature" rather than of the mind of Christ, we have at least defined the problem of ecumenical Christianity in its proper terms. This itself will be a great gain.

Thereafter, we shall not be able to make a virtue of our sectarianism, as every denomination has done in the past.

We shall not be able to glorify the founders of our denominations as having been led of God to establish their sectarian "churches" and so to divide Christ and his church. We may condone their action as due not alone to their "human nature," but quite as much to the "human nature" of the body from which they withdrew or which thrust them out by excommunication, but we cannot glory in what was done. If it is "human nature" that underlies our sectarianism and "justifies" it, the root of the thing is laid bare. Christianity has a name for it; its name is *sin*. Our denominational "churches" are the fruit of sin, and their continuance is a continuing in sin. Christianity knows only one thing to do with sin: it must be repented of, turned away from. The Protestant conscience which affirms the Lordship of Christ will have no rest until it turns away from the evil of its sectarianism and finds its true fellowship in the ecumenical community of which alone Christ is the living head.

Fortunately, however, the case does not need to rest here. For these sectarian churches do themselves give evidence that "human nature," touched by a little divine grace, is not incompatible with an ecumenical fellowship. The ideal of an ecumenical church resting alone on the Lordship of Christ can hardly be regarded as fantastic when it is found to be exemplified, despite their sectarian isolationism, in the denominational "churches" themselves. All these "churches," in their contemporary life, make room for diversity and disagreement in the very matters that formerly would have caused division. Most of our denominations no longer find their unity in an agreement upon those issues which historically occasioned their founding as separate "churches." Few of them, and none of the major ones, represent collectively a common mind on these issues. In the sense that they include in their membership and ministry a wide divergence of theological and ecclesiological conviction, they may even be said to be, so far forth, ecumenical. There are conservatives and liberals, conformists and dissenters, strict constructionists and latitudinarians, literalistic "fundamentalists" and profound fundamentalists, in all our denominations.

Do Episcopalians all see alike on the episcopacy? They do not. Do they all see alike on the sacraments, or the ministry, or even on the historic episcopate? No. The very premises upon which the standardized conception of these matters is based are challenged in the most iconoclastic manner by large sections of the Episcopal communion, including some of the most outstanding scholars and ecclesiastics, among them not a few bishops. It is little short of humorous for an advocate of "high church" doctrine or practice to proclaim the thesis that his particular doctrine of the church, the episcopate and the sacraments is essential to an ecumenical church, in face of the fact that his own "church" is a living demonstration of a fellowship which includes the widest diversity of opinion on all these subjects. Why should anyone wish to impose upon the ecumenical church a more rigorous conformity and unanimity than prevails in his own denomination?

Do Presbyterians all see alike on the Westminster Confession? By no means. There is wide divergence of doctrinal views, ranging from the most wooden-minded conformity to a strong belief that the classic standard requires radical revision, while not a few hold that it should be laid on the shelf as a historical symbol, rather than used as a present witness to the things Presbyterians believe. In thus including in its fellowship these diversities on matters once held to be crucial and fundamental, the Presbyterian Church is, so far forth, ecumenical. What was once held to be constitutive and constitutional for this denomination is now being released from the constitution and brought into the fellowship where diverse views are freely held and exchanged without ecclesiastical penalty for the dissenter.

Do all Baptists and all Disciples of Christ see alike on immersion-baptism? Far from it. Their arguments in support of it have undergone radical revision in the minds of large groups in both denominations. The thesis that "baptism" and "immersion" are equivalent terms is still maintained, but there are many to whom such a thesis is profoundly repugnant. Such persons continue to support the administration of baptism *by* immersion while rejecting the doctrine that the immersion *is* the baptism. It is true that in both of these denominations there exists a persistent threat of rupture over disagreements on this and other matters of biblical interpretation. Neither Baptists nor Disciples have gone so far in the withdrawal of doctrinal beliefs from the *constitution* of their denominations and the commitment of such matters to the *fellowship,* as have some of their neighbors, but the development of the inclusive and ecumenical ideal is distinctly under way.

Do all Congregationalists, all Baptists and all Disciples see alike on the "congregationalism" that formerly characterized their three denominations? Definitely no. Genuine differences exist in each group on the question of the absolute autonomy of the local church. Some still adhere to the belief that the New Testament knows no church other than the local congregation. Others strongly affirm that the primitive church was ecumenical (and this in the ecclesiastical sense) from the beginning, and that their several denominational traditions were mistaken in rejecting forms of connectional organization to express this ecumenical reality. The Congregationalists have, perhaps, gone farther in recognizing this ecclesiastical interdependence of local churches than have Baptists and Disciples. But in all three bodies the dogma of unqualified congregational autonomy is being withdrawn from its historic status in the constitutions of these denominations and is increasingly passing into the fellowship for free and tolerant re-examination.

These are only samples of the general movement toward a more ecumenical spirit within the sectarian "churches" themselves. I have not referred to the Methodist denomination because, being the least creedal-minded of all our larger bodies, it has, from its beginning, made room in its fellowship for an ecumenical diversity in theological opinion. Nor have I referred to Lutheranism which, in some of its American branches, is more rigorous in the use of its dogmas as constitutive of the church than other Protestant groups, and thus less ecumenical. But there are other branches of Lutheranism in which the ecumenical spirit is reducing doctrinal questions arising in the Lutheran tradition from their fixed constitutional status to the liberty of the Christian fellowship.

The denominations noted are sufficient to demonstrate the fact that "human nature" in the Christian church does not require separate denominational "churches" in order to hold and maintain diversity of convictions on doctrinal, ethical and ecclesiological questions. If this diversity can exist in the fellowship of a sectarian "church," there is no reason why it cannot obtain in the fellowship of the ecumenical church whose sole constitutive principle is the Lordship of Christ. Indeed, there is every reason to believe that, in an ecumenical church so constituted, the differences in the realm of opinion will almost automatically drop down from their constitutional status, where they now affront and deny the Lordship of

Christ, to the level of the free fellowship under Christ where they can be examined in the spirit of intellectual and conceptual liberty—the spirit wherewith Christ himself has made his church free.

How shall we account for this enlarging hospitality to wide diversities of doctrinal, ethical and ecclesiastical convictions in all the denominations? There are, of course, many answers. One answer, and an obvious one, lies in the fact that the mind of all the "churches" has been more or less penetrated by the spirit of enlightened scholarship which has given the modern mind a new understanding of the nature of the Bible, a new cosmos and a new outlook on history. The result is that the dogmas held tenaciously in the classical period when our denominations were formed, now sit more lightly on the mind of the "churches" or have passed entirely out of the category of dogma into that of direct insight. But this is only half of the answer, and the lesser half.

The other and the greater half is that, concomitantly with modern enlightenment, the Figure of Jesus Christ has emerged as the sole constitutive authority in his church. So long as his followers were under the delusion that the church must be constituted by dogmatic agreements, the face of Christ was obscured and his Lordship subordinated to the Bible or tradition or speculative theology. But today he is seen more clearly than at any time since the last apostle died. Fellowship with him and with all whom he has received into his church thus has tended with silent and irresistible power to transcend all sectarian distinctiveness and to create the beginning of an ecumenical consciousness in every denomination. This increasingly weakens the constitutional basis upon which our denominations are founded. It is now felt to be grossly incongruous with the mind of Christ to confront an applicant for membership in any of our denominations with any test of fellowship in terms of his doctrinal acceptance of the "standards" of the denomination. It is sufficient that he confess his faith in Christ and declare his purpose to lead a Christian life. Even in the ordination of a minister, the test to which he is subjected has less and less to do with his doctrinal "soundness" than with his personal devotion to Christ and the church.

We have here the mark of a great change in the interior spirit of most of our sectarian "churches." I have called it the ecumenical spirit—an ecumenical spirit in the sectarian "church" itself! It is the spirit of Phillips Brooks, inspiring prophet of this new day, who declared: "To me, the gospel is just one great Figure standing with outstretched arms." It is the spirit of Martin Luther who strongly desired the Protestant Reformation to rest, not upon the Bible or upon any other foundation than "the forgiving love of God in Christ." In Christ alone and in his Lordship, we have the sole constitutive principle of the Christian church.

The Bible is not constitutive of the church; it is the product of the church; it flowered in the fellowship of the church; its true place is forever in the fellowship, not in the constitution, of the church. So also with the creeds. They, too, arose within the fellowship; to use them to divide the fellowship of Christ's body into innumerable sectarian "churches" is apostasy from Christ. And the Protestant conscience in all our denominations confesses that it is aware of its apostasy by the blush of shame with which it rejects the thought that Christ is the head of its own denomination.

This new ecumenical spirit cannot be long contained in the ecclesiastical forms of the sectarian order. It is new wine and is already bursting the old bottles of sectarian exclusiveness. It demands a new ecclesiastical order of inclusiveness and comprehension, embracing all who acknowledge the Lordship of Christ. Such an order can be attained only by drawing clearly the distinction between the constitution of the church and the fellowship of the church. The constitution is forever determined by Christ himself. The fellowship is free, open to diversities and growth in the realm of doctrine, biblical interpretation, church order and procedure. That such an ecumenical Protestantism is possible is no longer a fantastic dream. Nor does it now rest entirely on faith. Its possibility is already being demonstrated in most of the denominations themselves. If it is possible in the Methodist, the Presbyterian, the Episcopal and many other "churches," where it has grown up imperceptibly, there can be no argument against its possibility on an ecumenical scale when it is projected consciously and deliberately under the urgent imperative of the mind of Christ.

In the whole range of controversial issues, I can think of only two sectarian features which would offer even a momentary problem for a Protestantism that is devoutly concerned to be ecumenical. One is the exclusive practice of baptism by immersion; the other, the exclusive ordination of ministers within the historic episcopate. But the first can be easily reconciled in an ecumenical church by the recognition of the full Christian status of those otherwise baptized and their acceptance by any local church without rebaptism. The second is really not so difficult as it has been made by the inflexible position of those on both sides. Protestantism in general has no convictions that should inhibit its acceptance of the historic episcopate, for every denomination has its own shorter-lived and less impressive, but still historic, episcopate. By some such procedure as the so-called "South India Plan," or the still better plan which Episcopalians and Presbyterians are now studying, the historic episcopate could, within a generation, become the possession of an ecumenical Protestantism.*

The authority of Christ cannot be invoked by the Protestant conscience in support of any denominational "church" in existence. A particular interpretation of the Bible can be

* Since this chapter appeared in the *Christian Century,* I have received a letter from Principal William Robinson of Overdale College, Birmingham, England, who directs attention to the practice of infant baptism as presenting a more difficult problem even than the practice of baptism by immersion. He says:

"You say quite rightly that only two things present even a momentary problem for a Protestantism that is devoutly concerned to be ecumenical: (1) the exclusive practice of baptism by immersion and (2) the exclusive ordination of ministers within the historic episcopate. But are you fully right about the first? I constantly find in American writers of Disciple and Baptist persuasion reference to baptism as if it were a matter only of the symbolism of the rite. Surely this is a minor matter compared with the question of whether baptism ought to be administered to infants or to believers. If you lived in this country you would realize it more. Here infant baptism is still indiscriminate and is practiced by most people, Christian and pagan. The infant is baptized just as it is vaccinated and there is a good deal of superstition attached to the rite. Marriage in church or burial in churchyard is not possible without this badge.

"This is a question which is fundamental to Protestantism. It goes to the roots of the matter. Is Christianity a magical or semi-magical religion? So long as the baptismal service of the Prayer Book stands, where baptism is quite rightly conceived as incorporation into Christ and into the church, and so long as baptism is administered to infants, this problem will remain. On the other hand, so long as Baptists resist this full meaning of the rite, and Baptists and Disciples do nothing about infants, it will remain.

"You go on to suggest that in the case of episcopal ordination the South India scheme points a way out. May I suggest that a similar way out might be sought for the baptismal controversy; that during an interim period all baptisms (infant and believers') might be accepted while at the same time some service for the blessing of infants be introduced and baptism and confirmation deferred until years of discretion. The question of the symbolism of baptism (immersion or sprinkling) would, I think, settle itself."

Principal Robinson has directed attention to a real problem which is now coming into the focus of theological consideration in pedobaptist as well as Baptist circles. His solution is essentially of the same character as that which I have indicated for the problem of immersion-baptism.

invoked, a particular creed can be invoked, a historic episcopate can be invoked, as a reason for maintaining schismatic "churches," but the authority of Christ cannot be invoked in justification of any of them. When it is invoked, the Protestant conscience has to confess that the lesser loyalties on which every such "church" is based are purely human ideologies and pragmatic functions in dealing with which the authority of Christ has left his church free. The only church which Christ recognizes as his, is the ecumenical church of the whole Christian community. Protestants, despite their inconsistency, willingly declare that this church alone is entitled to bear his name. Virtually all the "churches" of Christendom share this view, though with varying degrees of reservation. Rome alone rejects it.

To summarize: The ecumenical church of Christ is in an anomalous plight as the result of sectarianism. It exists, but it does not function! It does not function, because it has no organs through which its sovereign Head can exercise his divine purpose in his church. It has no organs, because they have all been stripped from it by sectarian egotism and are being exercised by separatistic "churches" none of which, by their own confession, is recognized by him as his church. Thus the true church of Christ is left impotent, a body without organs. Only as these false "churches" give back to his church the functions which they have usurped can Christ exercise his sovereign authority in a manner commensurate with the enormous responsibility which the world of today lays upon the Christian faith.

~ XV ~

THE DEMOCRACY OF THE SPIRIT

THE PROTESTANT mind will be under the constraint of powerful inhibitions as it contemplates the prospect of yielding its sectarian system to an ecumenical church. It has been long accustomed to assume that any variation from accepted doctrine justified the founding of a new "church" to propagate and exemplify it. The "churches" will hesitate to give up this sectarian "right." They will fear for the fate of their own cherished doctrines, their biblical interpretations and their ecclesiastical apparatus in an ecumenical church constituted on so broad a basis as that on which Christ has constituted his church. What, it will be asked, will happen to these particular treasures if, instead of their being fixed in the constitution of a special "church," they are left to the free forum of the spiritual democracy of the ecumenical church?

The answer is multiple. (1) You may lose some of them and you may be glad to lose them when the light of free inquiry and discussion reveals how empty they are. (2) You may be surprised to find how acceptable to your fellow Christians some of them are, now that the label of your exclusive sectarian patent on them has been removed. (3) You will find yourself actually taking over from others their treasures of thought and Christian experience, and even some of their ecclesiastical procedures and ways of worship, whose value you have not appreciated while you were living in the isolated provincialism of your sectarian "church." (4) There will be some opinions of yours which you cannot persuade others to receive at your hands, and some belonging to others which you cannot adopt or approve—but that is the way it is in your own sectarian "church," is it not? Is it right to ask more unanimity and uniformity in the ecumenical church than you have in your sectarian "church"?

An Ecumenical Theology

The same question will be pressed in another and still more radical form: Will not an ecumenical Protestantism, founded on no other constitutive principle than the Lordship of Christ, tend toward latitudinarianism? If the doctrines are not fixed in the constitution of the church, but freely committed to its fellowship, will not the theological content of the Christian faith tend to give way to a vague sentimentalism or to mere moralism, thus sacrificing the intellectual substance of Christianity? Such an outcome, I agree, would be deplorable. But the fear expressed in such questions is groundless. The intellectual content of the Christian faith has never been protected or advanced by writing creeds into the constitutions of sectarian "churches," nor will it be advanced by writing a creed into the constitution of the ecumenical church. On the contrary, Christian truth has been distorted and cheapened by this procedure.

The arrogance of the claim to finality and infallibility in the realm of Christian belief has raised barriers against the natural circulation of Christian truth both within the church as a whole and in the world outside. So long as the Christian ideology is divided up and dispersed in the sectarian pigeon-

holes of Protestantism, it cannot command attention on its
intrinsic merits. Not only does it encounter prejudice in its
attempt to gain entrance into other sectarian mentalities than
its own, but it encounters an impenetrable prejudice, not to
say contempt, when it is offered to the intelligence of the
intellectual world.

The fact is that the vitality of Christian truth has historically been conserved and its growth fostered in spite of the
existence of sectarian boundaries. These boundaries have
hindered but have not wholly suppressed this free movement
of Christian thought. The great minds that have powerfully
influenced the church's thinking have always transcended
denominational limitations. The light of their insights, though
impeded by the existing sectarian fixations, travels across
denominational lines and tends to become the possession of
the whole church. That is to say, theological progress already
proceeds in the limited spiritual democracy that we now have
despite our ecclesiastical separateness. This is more true today
than ever before. Christian truth is in the way of becoming
ecumenical. It makes its way in the medium of the intellectual
democracy that is breaking through the walls of the creedal
and theological authoritarianism of the sects. And instead of
its becoming latitudinarian, the dominant trend of Christian
theology today is toward a specifically, distinctively and
uniquely Christian body of thought.

With the removal of the walls of sectarian churchism which
now clutter the terrain of the ecumenical church and hinder
the free activity of Christian thought, we may expect an ecumenical theology consciously to emerge as such. Such a
theology will have a new power and dignity and will command respect in our science-minded world which now treats
our sectarianized creeds with levity. In the free exercise of

Christian intelligence, under Christ, in the spiritual democracy of the Christian fellowship, the Holy Spirit will, no doubt, confirm much that is old—much more, I believe, than the latitudinarians imagine. And the same Spirit will guide the mind of the fellowship in the perennial discovery of those things which Christ withheld from his disciples until the Spirit should reveal them.

Let us pursue the matter of the Spirit's guidance a little further. Why should any Christian shrink from entrusting the truth of Christianity to the democracy of the ecumenical fellowship? Is not that precisely where Christ himself left it? The early church had no thought of standardizing and codifying Christian truth, or of its right to do so. In John's Gospel we have the clear evidence of its sense of freedom in the search for truth. The church claimed no authority, but it claimed *guidance*. Christ is reported as having committed his truth to the keeping of the whole Christian community. "I have much more to tell you," he said, on the evening of his departure from his disciples, "but you cannot take it in now; but when the Spirit of Truth comes, he will guide you into all truth."

Imagine one of our Protestant sectarians as a member of this company of disciples. He would have trembled for the future of the Christian faith as he heard these words of his Master. He would have advised Jesus that this was a terrible risk; that his cause was precarious and probably hopeless unless he would now set forth in authoritative form what his disciples must believe; or promise an infallible book for their guidance; or at least name a committee from the group to draft a creed in his name after he had gone. But Jesus had no such thought. Instead, he talked to them of the Spirit that would guide them into a fuller understanding of his mind, only a small part of which he had been able to lay bare. In effect, he said that the whole community of believers—that is, the Christian church—was to be the bearer and only "custodian" of the truth, and it was to receive the truth under the perpetual guidance of the Spirit.

To be unwilling to entrust the truth of the Christian faith to the ecumenical intelligence of the church under the guidance of the Spirit, and to demand that the free flow of thought be arrested and codified in authoritative and constitutional creeds, betrays an attitude of unfaith. The ark of God needs no such steadying hand. Christian truth will take care of itself if it is not bound by these human infallibilities. The surest cure for every heresy short of the repudiation of the Lordship of Christ, is not summarily to excommunicate it, but to give it hospitality in the spiritual and intellectual democracy of the Christian community. Besides, it will often turn out that a little fellowship with heresy is a wholesome corrective of hidden error. Only an ecumenical theology can be a sound Christian theology. And an ecumenical theology requires the free and undivided participation of the whole church in the perennial exploration of the mind of Christ under the guidance of the Spirit.

CHURCH ORDER—A SPIRITUAL DEMOCRACY

Not only in the realm of Christian belief has the church been left free to seek the truth under the guidance of the Spirit, but it has also been left free to implement itself with an order or polity by the exercise of its own intelligence under the guidance of the same Spirit. Whatever theological doctrine one may hold as to the *nature* of the Holy Spirit,* the *function* of the Spirit and the *method* of its manifestation is

---

*I personally hold to an essentially trinitarian doctrine.

clear. There is nothing magical or supernatural or weird about the way in which it manifests itself in the church. The operation of the Spirit is more familiar than is commonly supposed. It is as familiar as the common practice of democracy. Indeed, the guidance of the Spirit is the Christian counterpart of the principle of democracy. Perhaps it is better to put it the other way around and say that the principle of democracy in the secular order is the political counterpart of the same principle in the Christian church. In the church, the principle of democracy attains its most exalted conception and manifestation, because it is the method by which the Spirit of God operates in the community of those who remember and love and honor Jesus Christ.

But there is a difference between the democracy of the church and the political practice of democracy. This difference derives from the fact that the church is a sacramental community, and its democracy partakes of the sacramental character which is of the essence of the church itself. All the functions of the church, its communal worship, its offices and ordained office-bearers, its councils and conventions and committees, its offerings, its missions, its benevolences, down to the practical details of administering its affairs—all are sacramental. They are made sacramental by the presence of the Holy Spirit. The idea that the church has only two sacraments, baptism and the Lord's Supper, is heresy. The idea that sacramental grace has been exclusively committed to an authoritative hierarchy to be dispensed to the faithful, is an execrable heresy. Sacramental grace is the possession of the whole Christian community. The church itself is a sacramental brotherhood. In it every member participates on a spiritual parity with every other member—Jew and Greek and barbarian, bond and free, male and female.

The institutional or organizational aspect of this community consists merely of the correlated offices or organs through which this sacramental community functions. And every office-bearer, be he called bishop, presbyter, priest, minister, pastor, deacon or whatever, derives the function of his office and receives his ordination to it from the sacramental community of the Holy Spirit whose representative he is.

In this spiritual democracy there is no place for the exercise of any irresponsible authority. All offices and organs, and those who administer them, operate only under an indissoluble responsibility to the Christian community. Yet not even is the community itself sovereign. Christ alone, its living Head, is sovereign. And the will of Christ is made known to the church by its dependence upon the Spirit which is immanent in the devotion and intelligence of the community. This is the distinguishing mark of the spiritual democracy of the church as compared with political democracy or the intellectual democracy of science. It is like them, but it is different. Both of these expressions of the democratic principle are caught up into the church, but they are exalted into another dimension by the Spirit. In contrast with political democracy, the dependence of the church upon the Spirit demands the rejection of the idea of the ultimate sovereignty of the community and saves it from the temptation to adopt the *vox populi, vox dei* fallacy. In contrast with the democracy of science, the dependence of the church upon the Spirit saves its intelligence from intellectual egotism and humanism in its pursuit of the truth.

The picture I have drawn is, unhappily, not a photograph, but a freehand sketch of the Christian ideal. A photograph of contemporary Protestantism would show how far short of this ideal it has fallen. A photograph of Romanism would show that it has utterly perverted this ideal and abandoned it. Rome has robbed the spiritual democracy of the Christian community of its democratic function and substituted a monarchical dictatorship for the democracy of the Spirit. The difference between the two photographs is, in one aspect, not great, but in another aspect it is profound. Both Rome and Protestantism alike have rejected the Holy Spirit—Rome, in its usurpation of the spiritual democracy of the Christian community by a monarchical hierarchy; Protestant sectarianism, by dividing the Spirit into separated "churches," thus curtailing its full manifestation and function.

The Spirit of God is the ecumenical Spirit. It belongs to the whole church, not to a part of it. And much less to a professional class empowered to impart its benefits. It can fully function in accordance with its divine nature only in the fellowship and through the organs of the whole ecumenical community. But these organs and functions have been usurped by sectarian fragments of the community and exercised as if each fragment was the whole church of Christ; with the result that the body of Christ has been left impotent, having neither organs nor functions through which the Spirit can operate according to its nature. In this aspect, Protestant sectarianism has done what Rome does—it has usurped the functions of the spiritual democracy of the Christian community.

Nevertheless, the ideal picture I have sketched is, in another aspect, essentially a true Protestant picture. For, despite their sectarian usurpation of ecumenical prerogatives, all Protestant sects, within their sectarian framework, pay tribute to the principle of a spiritual democracy. In America, at least, there is no evangelical Protestant body, from the Episcopalians to the Quakers, that is other than intentionally democratic in its organizational procedures. In respect to interior structure or polity, not one of these "churches" clothes any office or office-bearer with irresponsible authority within its sectarian framework. It is the intention of each one to maintain the democratic principle and, though the Spirit's guidance is restricted in such a framework, it is, nevertheless, consciously sought.

There is, of course, a wide diversity of forms among these so-called "churches," ranging all the way from the Episcopalians, the Presbyterians, the Lutherans and the Methodists at one end of the line, to those representing a congregational polity, such as the Congregationalists, the Baptists and the Disciples, at the other extreme. But all claim to exemplify the principle of democracy. If I yield to the prompting to express an opinion on the relative merits of their several claims, it will not be an expression of sectarian prejudice. Though I myself belong to a denomination which almost makes a fetish of its congregational independence and autonomy, and imagines that this polity is the very essence of democracy, I feel bound to say that this is a delusion; and to add that this state of mind presents one of the most formidable obstacles to the realization of an ecumenical Protestantism. Certain it is that an ecumenical Protestantism cannot be conceived as a vast multitude of dispersed local churches each insisting upon its autonomy and independence in relation to all the others. This would be the absolute opposite of an ecumenical church.

As a theory of church polity, congregationalism is not a good illustration of the spiritual democracy of the church of Christ, but a partial denial of it. Its local churches are not in fact really independent. They inevitably acknowledge some degree of organic interdependence. As an ecclesiastical theory, congregationalism is a heresy. Not only has it no support in the New Testament, but it is denied in practice by the denominations which hold it. In so far as their local churches are integrated in cooperative undertakings and conventions under the concept of identifiable denominations—Baptist, Disciples or Congregational—they pay tribute, however grudgingly, to the *corporate* existence of their denomination. Their local churches are the expression, each in its own particular place, of the denomination whose prior existence is responsible for their being there.

To imagine that this theory of absolute congregational autonomy can be carried over into the ecumenical church is an illusion. The ecumenical church cannot be conceived as the *sum* of its local units. It exists prior to them all. It is greater than them all, greater than the sum of them. Each local church is the expression in its own particular place of the overarching ecumenical church without whose prior existence it would not be there. No appeal to the New Testament can support this extreme congregationalism. The Christian church was ecumenical from the beginning. The New Testament distinctly discloses the objective reality of *the church,* as distinguished from the local churches, and a profound sense of the whole church as a corporate body. This inevitably led, even before the end of the New Testament period, to the emergence of an incipient corporate framework or order. No New Testament writer deplores or condemns this development. And there is no reason to doubt that, in principle, if not in form, it occurred under the guidance of the Spirit.

We have, then, two general theories of church organization in Protestantism—the corporate or organic, and the congregational. Which of these conceptions best expresses the spiritual democracy of the Christian fellowship? I have said that all Protestant denominations in America are committed to the democratic principle in their polity or order. This is in contrast with the monarchical principle of Rome. But there are these two types of polity represented at one end of the Protestant scale by such bodies as the Episcopalian, Presbyterian, Lutheran and Methodist denominations, and at the other end by such bodies as Baptists, Disciples and Congregationalists. All adhere to the democratic principle in their intention. Which group of "churches" is, in fact, the more democratic? Which group gives the larger place for the spiritual democracy of their own sectarian "churches" to express itself deliberately and unitedly under the guidance of the Spirit? It is absolutely essential to answer this question if there is to be any meeting of minds on an ecumenical level. There is no middle ground between these two concepts, although there is considerable middle ground for varying structure and procedure under both.

The movement toward an ecumenical Protestantism has reached the point where it can no longer evade this issue. It is a practical question to be resolved in the freedom of the Christian fellowship by Christian intelligence under the guidance of the Spirit. In its consideration, the democratic *intention* of none of these denominations can be challenged. What can be argued is whether one or the other concept provides the fullest freedom for the exercise of the spiritual democracy of the Christian community.

The Episcopalian, speaking for his group of "churches," will deplore the disorder, the lack of disciplined responsibility, the exposure to fanaticism, secularism, localism and ambitious self-appointed leadership which he sees in the other group of "churches." In a word, the Episcopalian will say that the congregational sort of democracy lacks the *representative* principle with its checks and balances which the democratic principle as applied to a large body always needs both for its self-discipline and for its most deliberate self-expression.

Therefore, he may argue, the type of democracy represented by congregationalism is insufficient for an ecumenical church.

The Baptist, speaking for his group, will deplore the over-weighting of the ecclesiastical apparatus of the other group of "churches," their restraint on religious spontaneity, their constant exposure to the peril of formalism and their tendency toward sacerdotalism in which he sees a disguised authoritarianism. All of this, he will argue, is repressive of the spiritual democracy of the Christian fellowship, and therefore the type of democracy represented by the denominations with a corporate polity is insufficient for an ecumenical church.

In such an exchange of views, the other "churches" of each group will have their say, and the sharp issue drawn between the two ecclesiastical theories by the more extreme representatives of each will be modified. Is it possible that a *modus vivendi* can be achieved which will guard the ecumenical church against the anarchic irresponsibility of extreme congregational theory, on the one hand, and the overweighted apparatus of organization resulting in the repression of spiritual spontaneity on the other? I believe it is possible. But it is possible only if the problem is translated out of the terms of dogma and tradition and biblical authority into the terms of a spiritual democracy seeking, under the guidance of the Spirit, to implement its fellowship for the greatest efficiency and the fullest expression of its own life.

The patient reader who has followed me thus far has a right to ask whether there has been in the author's mind any imagery of such an ecumenical church, however vague and tentative, by which his writing of this book has been guided. The request is a fair one, and deserves a candid response. In general, I have sought to avoid suggesting anything like a blueprint of an ecumenical structure, but have confined myself to an analysis of the Protestant situation in the belief that such an analysis would yield the principles along which the goal of an ecumenical church might be cooperatively envisaged. The structure of the ecumenical church cannot be envisaged in advance by any of us. But I am willing to confess that all my thought from beginning to end has been accompanied by a tentative image of the kind of church that will answer to the desperate demand for an ecumenical Protestantism. If the Episcopal Church would let the ecumenical church have its bishops and its historic episcopate without the sacerdotalism of the "apostolic succession," and the Baptists, Disciples and Congregationalists would contribute their principle of congregational freedom, modified and disciplined by the principle of congregational interdependence and responsibility—if these were contributed to and received by the whole church, it would be a matter of relative indifference whether the structure—that is, the polity or order—of the ecumenical church were fashioned on the model of any one of the Episcopal-Presbyterian-Lutheran-Methodist group of churches. Other denominations besides those I have named would have their appropriate contributions to make, but I think they will agree that, in general terms, they are included in one or another of the categories represented by those I have mentioned.

Many Christians are timid when they contemplate the prospect of an organic ecumenical Protestantism. This is because they are unable to envisage any other form of a united Protestantism except that with which they are familiar in the authoritarian structure of the Roman Church. They see no alternative to such a hierarchical institution save to continue their present denominational divisions. Naturally, therefore, they shrink from any effort that looks toward the strengthening of Protestantism as a whole.

But the possibilities of organization which inhere in the democratic principle are multiple. None of us is competent to determine in advance the particular form which, out of the numerous possibilities, the collective mind of Protestantism, intent on unity, would adopt. Of one thing we may be sure: an organic Protestant unity would be the exact opposite of the unity of Roman Catholicism. It would not be authoritarian; it could be only democratic.

Nor need we fear that an ecumenical Protestantism would be so large as to be unwieldy. The democratic principle lends itself to wide flexibility in its application. Under this principle the legitimate autonomy of the local churches could be faithfully conserved in a regional or synodical or diocesan structure whose functions would be derived from the consent of the local churches of the particular region or synod or diocese. The "organic" unity need not extend beyond these regional or synodical or diocesan units. These units could be larger or smaller—their size would be determined by the principle of practical efficiency. (This flexibility as to size is what I have in mind in using three alternative terms—regional, synodical or diocesan.)

If the diocesan unit is adopted, as it quite certainly would be, the dioceses could then be united in some regional or synodical structure, possibly one that is co-terminous with the boundaries of our several states. There is nothing unwieldy about such a form of unity. The local churches would fit snugly into it. It would be their own creation by their democratic consent, and its control would rest democratically in their hands.

These regional or synodical units, spread over the whole

nation, could be united nationally by the federal principle in a Federal Council. Its functions would be not unlike those now exercised by the Federal Council of Churches—but with this difference: the Federal Council of a united Protestantism would not be a federation of *denominational "churches,"* but a federation of autonomous geographical units of an undenominational Protestantism which, within these units, would be organically united.

Thus, by taking over the federal principle from the present denominational structure and utilizing it as the principle of cooperation and common witness of a united Protestantism, the legitimate autonomy of the local churches and their connectional units would be conserved and guarded all the way along—from the local church itself through the united diocesan and/or regional unit, to the federalized functioning of the whole body of united Protestantism at the national level. In such a democratic organization of Protestantism—"organic" at the bottom and federated at the top—there would be no risk of either authoritarianism or unwieldiness. Indeed, it would be farther removed from these dangers than is the case in many of our denominations at the present time.

I have allowed myself to go into more detail than I had intended in expressing my personal concept of the possible form which an ecumenical Protestantism might assume. But I could hardly do less, in all candor, than to disclose to the reader the concrete picture that has flitted in and out of my mind the while I have been writing these chapters.

The Fellowship of the Spirit

It may seem that, throughout this book, our attention has been so focused upon the organizational aspect of Protestantism—its present divisions, their folly, their weakness and their dishonor to Christ, and the imperative need of attaining an organic ecumenical Protestantism—that I have been betrayed into the fallacy of supposing that mere organizational strength, great enough to match the massive blocs of secularism and the firmly integrated dictatorship of Roman Catholicism, is all that is required for Protestantism to win America and the world to the Christian faith. If any reader has gained such an impression, let him be assured that I hold no such superficial and fallacious notion.

I insist again that the ecumenical church, if it is to have any real and empirical existence, must have a body with organs and functions. Otherwise it exists only as an idea, an ideal, perhaps only as a dream. But the motive for the attainment of such a church is a double one—not only to bring to bear the full strength of the Christian faith upon the objective scene in America and throughout the world, but also to enrich and greaten the spiritual life of every individual Christian believer. The Christian man cannot come to his full stature in Christ in a church that divides the spiritual democracy of Christ into exclusive sectarian "churches." His sectarian "church" cheats him of his full Christian heritage. "All are yours," said St. Paul, as he strove to inhibit the budding threat of sectarian divisions in the Corinthian church—"all are yours, whether Paul or Apollos or Cephas; all are yours and ye are Christ's." The Apostle foresaw the impoverishment of spiritual life that sectarianism would entail, and admonished the Corinthians to remain ecumenical in order that they might have the full richness of Christian experience which only the ecumenical fellowship could supply.

The individual Christian will experience a profound enrichment of his spiritual life as the result of his belonging to a church that is worthy of his heart-whole allegiance. As his consciousness of belonging only to a fragment of the church gives way to the consciousness of belonging to the whole church of Christ, his very soul will be inexpressibly enlarged. His Christian faith and allegiance will be exalted. The sense of futility and emptiness which now haunts his ever so faithful devotion to a sectarian fragment of the church of Christ, will vanish. His ardent devotion will then be given, under Christ, to a church whose solidarity and strength will command the respect in the world, in the nation and in the local community which the Lordship of Christ deserves and which sectarianism cannot evoke. Such an ecumenical Protestantism can confront the magnitudes of secular power with the power of the gospel of Christ and so discharge its responsibility for the character of the national life and of world civilization. And every believer will be a participant in this great and holy brotherhood. The glory of its world-wide mission and the depths of its richer fellowship will be reflected in his own soul. As an ecumenical Christian, his membership in the whole church will be invested with a dignity, a sense of reality, of meaning and of certain triumph which the decaying significance of denominational "churches" and the parochial-mindedness of their local congregations can no longer provide.

Thus the attainment of an ecumenical church by modern Protestantism will actually produce *a new kind of Christian*. Those who piously insist that action toward the reconstruction of Protestantism must wait until we have a profound change in the spiritual life of Protestant church members are only rationalizing their own unwillingness to act. Nothing less than the reconstruction of Protestantism will evoke the spiritual life they desiderate!

There is enough—barely enough—spiritual life in the denominational "churches" to bring the ecumenical church into functioning existence. Action in this realm need not wait upon an access of spirituality. There will never be any more spiritual vitality in the denominational "churches" than we now have. These "churches" have long since passed their zenith in spiritual vigor, as they have also in their competence to win America. The two are correlative—a competent church and a vital spiritual life. They go down together, and have been going down together for two or three generations. But they also go up together—the corporate competence of Protestantism to register the full strength of the Christian faith in the social order, and the quality of spiritual life expressed in personal devotion to Christ. The two interact with each other in a mutuality that is inseparable.

Therefore the attainment of an ecumenical church is in the interest of a profounder, a richer and a more adequate Christian experience in personal life. The conscious undertaking of this high task will be profoundly felt in the soul of every individual Christian who shares in it. Those who long for a revival of grace and spiritual power in contemporary Protestantism—and who does not long for it?—will have their prayer answered by helping to remove the walls of sectarian division, thus setting free the spiritual democracy of the Christian fellowship in an ecumenical Protestantism.

It is futile to try to galvanize spiritual life into a revival heat within the sectarian "churches." These "churches" have already reached their maximum of spirituality in a system which is in a process of decay. Conventional evangelism in the medium of this system has long since worn itself out. Its apparent successes, gained under methods of high pressure, are illusory, ephemeral and barren. It can be affirmed with dogmatic assurance that there will be no "great awakening" in Protestantism until its leaders and its people set their hands and their hearts to the great task of giving to Christ the church which his divine Lordship deserves, for which he prayed and for whose life he died. What wonders he would work in and through such a church no tongue can tell.

~ XVI ~

THE UNFINISHED REFORMATION

THE PROTESTANT Reformation was a new and profoundly creative event in human history. It was not a passing episode. It was far more than a moral protest against the intolerable corruption then existing in the Roman Catholic Church. As a result of the pitiless exposure of this corruption by the reformers, the Roman Church was appreciably cleansed. But even a Roman Catholicism cleansed of its more flagrant and noisome corruption had then, and has now, no attraction for Protestantism. The Reformation severed for good and all every bond of connection with the hierarchical system by which the Roman Church is constituted.

Protestantism can never have ecclesiastical fellowship with a church which maintains itself as a system of irresponsible power derived from the abject submission of its members. It is such a system which is the essence of Roman Catholicism. It falsifies Christianity, is an affront to human dignity, is incompatible with both the spirit and the institutions of democracy, and contains within itself the ineradicable seeds of its own corruption. No such irresponsible power is safe in any human hands.

The Reformation was the emergence of a new order, based, not upon an ignoble submission to a self-constituted authority,

211

but upon the dignity of the individual man whose capacity to answer for himself directly to God it proclaimed as its fundamental principle. The respective bases of Roman Catholicism and Protestantism are thus mutual opposites. They are irreconcilable. No false tolerance fallaciously taken over from the political tolerance rightly prevailing in a democratic secular society should obscure their irreconcilability.

The creative moment which brought to birth the Protestant Reformation could hardly have occurred save as the times were ripe for it, save as the currents of history were converging toward it. Western civilization was involved in one of the two or three major crises of human history. The Renaissance had released the intellectual life of man from the repressive authority of the medieval church. The Holy Roman Empire had become a hollow shell and was giving way to the rising spirit of nationalism. The feudal economy was breaking up under the impact of a new method of trade, called capitalism. None of these forces was integral to Protestantism, but together they provided the circumstantial possibility of its emergence. They helped Protestantism to come into being, and left their marks upon it, not all, by any means, good.

Yet this seems to be the way God works in history. He sent his Son in the fullness of time—that is, at a moment when many forces and elements conspired to make the historical emergence of Christianity possible. Some of these quite extraneous factors left their marks upon primitive Christianity, not all, by any means, good. The Reformation, in its deepest thought, represented the resurgence of the essential Christianity that had long been distorted and repressed by the debased form which the Christian faith had taken on in the Middle Ages.

But this resurgence appeared under historical circumstances which had no essential similarity to the historical circumstances in which original Christianity emerged. Every historical situation is, of course, unique. In the case of the Reformation, the uniqueness of its historical situation demands that Protestantism be discerned not only as the resurgence of something that had existed long before and had been smothered for centuries, namely, essential Christianity, but also as a new historical emergent opening a new epoch in the life of Christianity itself. Protestantism was something old; but it was also something new. Certainly the early Christians, could they have been called from their graves and set down in the midst of the Protestant Reformation, would have had considerable difficulty, amounting to bewilderment, in making themselves at home.

This element of originality or "novelty" in the Reformation, derived from its unique historical situation, helps us to understand the Protestant intention to make a complete break with Roman Catholicism. The particular circumstances of the sixteenth century placed Protestantism in the stream of historical destiny, and left the Roman Church stranded in feudal medievalism, where it remains today. In severing all connection with Rome, Protestantism had no intention of ever going back. It repudiated absolutely the "catholicity" of the Roman Catholic Church, and consigned that church, with sublime impudence, to the category of a sect, and an apostate one. It looked forward either (1) to the destruction of that church by the historical forces which its future would encounter, or (2) to its reform from within by the abandonment of its exercise of an irresponsible power derived from the practice of an indignity upon the human soul. But the reformers did not expect that such a reform would take place from within. Hence their definitive and irreversible break with Rome. Nor should we expect it. The power held by the professional class in the Roman Church, under the dictatorship of the papacy, is not likely to be given up voluntarily. History shows no instance where such power on so massive a scale has ever been willingly relinquished. Such a reform would require that the whole structure of that church be turned upside down and a new foundation laid in the immanent sovereignty of Christ and the dignity of man before God.

In Protestantism this "reform" has already occurred. The deepest intention of the Reformation was to break with the rule of the papacy, and to re-establish in the church the authority of Christ which would then be expressed, not through a human dictatorship, but through his immanent presence in the spiritual democracy of the Christian community. The Christian church itself, as an organic whole, is, in Protestantism, the true "vicegerent" of Christ on earth, and Christ exercises his function as head of the church, not in terms of some human "authority" or "power" proceeding from the top down, but through a living community disciplined by the Holy Spirit to maintain its organic unity under his immanent Lordship. This is the ecclesiological basis of an ecumenical Protestantism.

The tragedy of the Reformation lay in the fact that it did not complete its reform. It broke with Rome, but, unwittingly, it carried over in its sectarianism the very principle in Rome against which it had revolted. In magnifying liberty of interpretation, it forgot the discipline of Christ. It thus bred anarchy. Its anarchy coalesced in a multitude of infallibilities, each one decreeing that its interpretation of the Bible *was* the Bible, as Rome does, and therefore authorizing and justifying the erection of a "church"—"the true New Testament church"—upon its interpretation, as also Rome does. Yet all the while each such "church" cherished the belief that it was proceeding under the authority of Christ, because, forsooth, it derived its "church" from the Bible.

Protestant sectarianism, strangely, has never been aware that it was contradicting the authority of Christ and affronting him in building its "churches" on the Bible. The utter confusion and anarchy which this use of the Bible brought upon Protestantism should have caused it long since to challenge the principle upon which it was proceeding. One would suppose that Protestant intelligence could have discerned that something was radically wrong with a tree that brings forth such fruits. Yet despite its substitution of the authority of the Bible for the authority of Christ, Protestantism has unremittingly proclaimed its allegiance to the authority of Christ, and it has never yielded the ecumenical theory of itself as a spiritual democracy under his divine Lordship. But its spiritual democracy has failed to maintain its ecumenical character because the false use of the Bible eclipsed the sole authority upon which the ecumenical church is constituted, namely, the undelegated authority of Christ.

When Protestantism now affirms its ecumenical character it has to do so with its tongue in its cheek. In the back of its mind it knows that as a historical actuality it is not ecumenical. Rome can point to its more than two hundred denominational "churches" and, looking Protestantism fairly in the eye, can scornfully say: "These 'churches' belie your claim to be ecumenical. Your denominational 'churches' are, every one of them, little counterfeit imitations of Rome, resting upon the same kind of basis as that which you say caused you to leave the Roman Catholic Church, namely, an infallible interpretation of an infallible Bible. We have one vicegerent of Christ; you have more than two hundred." Every word of this indictment would be true; and the scorn with which it is spoken would be fully warranted.

To the question, "Can Protestantism Win America?" the initial answer, given in the seventh chapter, was that it can do so only as it confronts the contemporary scene as if the Christianization of America depended, under God, upon it alone. Protestantism, I have said, has no ally with which it can collaborate in this undertaking. The culture of America is destined to be, if not Protestant, either Roman Catholic or secular. Neither Roman Catholicism nor secularism is an ally of Protestantism; both are competitors of Protestantism for the soul of America. It is a waste of time and a dissipation of strength to court either of them. This can be said in the same breath with which it is reiterated that Protestantism will continue to maintain a spirit of tolerance in the political and social order toward other faiths and, in particular, toward Roman Catholicism and Judaism.

But Protestantism is weak. Secularism and Catholicism are strong. Each is entrenched in a formidable system of power for which Protestantism in its present state is no match. Potentially, however, Protestantism is strong—in numbers, in wealth, in the prestige of a long tradition intimately identified with America's culture and institutions. But it is prodigally wasting its preponderant numbers, its vast wealth and its unique prestige in a system that is no system, in which freedom has gone to seed because the Christian virtue of disciplined freedom under Christ has never come to consciousness as a moral imperative. In a word, Protestantism has refused to be an organism; it has maintained its existence in a dispersion of unrelated ecclesiastical cells. This is its weakness and its impotence as it confronts an American mentality gone secular and therefore, in the day of its spiritual disillusionment, peculiarly susceptible to the plausible appeal of Roman Catholicism.

Moreover, the significance and spiritual strength of the sectarian cells, which call themselves "churches," is now in a process of decay. Their historical claims of distinctively possessing some precious truth which justified their separate existence, are regarded with polite contempt by the general community and are maintained with increasing hollowness within the sectarian cells themselves. A corrosive moral insincerity pervades the whole denominational order of Protestantism. Its creeds and distinctive practices are evaded with ingenious casuistry, even at the ordination of its ministers, and are almost totally disregarded in the reception of new members. When its creeds and distinctive practices are referred to in informal conversation, and even in public address, it is often with an indulgent smile which may be accompanied either by a half-veiled apology or by a wisecrack.

This does not necessarily indicate that its creeds are untrue or unimportant or even that they are no longer believed. Of some of them, it is true that they are no longer believed; of others, that they are no longer held to be important, even if true; but of others it must be said that they are still held to be true and, as creeds, important. What, then, does the decay of the denominations mean? *It means that their "distinctive features" are no longer held as a sufficient reason for maintaining separate "churches" built upon them.* They are the common possession of Protestantism. By and large, they always were; and the recognition of this fact is coming home to the conscience of Protestantism with at least a pale sense of guilt. Christ himself refuses to recognize as his church any of the "churches" built upon such foundations.

Throughout these pages I have confined our outlook to the

American scene and have adhered strictly and even narrowly to the Protestant situation in America. But I have all along been haunted by the feeling that there was a certain unreality in dealing with both America and Protestantism within limits so narrowly prescribed. Virtually all that has been said could have been said many years ago. I have taken "America" for granted and "Protestantism" for granted in the setting in which they now exist and have existed for a long time. But neither America nor Protestantism can any longer be taken for granted. Both are now caught in a vast world convulsion. Civilization is in a state of collapse. The old stabilities have been dissolving before our eyes. The old world of America and of Protestantism is passing away. Whether a new world will rise from the chaos of the present, and whether, if it does, it will be better or worse than the world we have known, no man can tell. What the future holds for humanity is beyond our ken. Only faith in the God of history can enable us to ride the tempestuous waves of this universal unrest.

All this adds urgency to the need of a strong Protestantism. In the new era into which the world is passing, a task will confront Protestantism for which its historical character as a congeries of sectarian "churches" has left it tragically handicapped and unprepared. It can no longer complacently measure itself in terms of the longtime relatively stable order that is passing away. It must widen its horizon and think in terms of the future. It can face its future with intelligence only if it now sees itself in the perspective of the present world revolution and as an actual participant in it.

The very stresses of uncertainty under the shadow of an impenetrable and portentous future, should make it impossible for Protestantism to think small thoughts and to emphasize trivial things. It is an opportunity such as its "churches" were never before given to think in large categories and to attempt great things. If the end of our era proves to be like the end of other great eras in history, it may fall out that all that is left of civilization will be found in the keeping of the Christian church. The responsibility that will then rest upon Christianity will be staggeringly more obvious than the responsibility which it inherently carried in a stable and more favorable environment. The thought of carrying our impotent sectarianism into such a scene as that toward which the forces of history may be taking us, should give Protestantism a new criterion by which to measure its weaknesses and should powerfully reinforce its will to be strong. Thus transformed, perhaps it will not be called "Protestantism." I share with many the hope that its historical genius will find a new name for it, an ecumenical name answering to its long hidden ecumenical character and the ecumenical intention by which the Reformation was motivated.

Facing such a future pregnant with a new world not yet come to birth, Protestant Christianity faces also its own destiny. Either it will decay with the decaying significance of its sectarian "churches," as some believe it will, or a new Protestantism will emerge from its anarchic sectarianism as the true ECUMENICAL CHURCH OF CHRIST. Only such a church can provide the religious resources needed to gather up the fragments of a shattered civilization and with them build a new society. Only such a church can win the America that now is or the America that is to be, to the Christian faith. And it is only upon this faith that an enduring order of mankind can be built in America and in the new world that is struggling to be born.

INDEX

Aaron, 115

American culture: foundations of, 84; in 19th century, 11 ff., 50; today, 13 ff., 49, 78, 82-83; and public schools, 8, 19

American mind: *See* Collectivist mind . . .

A.P.A., 61

Apostles, authority of, 139-40

Apostles' Creed, 103

Apostolic succession, 171, 189 f., 204

Aristophanes, 52

Arnold, Matthew, 91 n.

Art, 55 ff.

Association of Catholic Trades Unionists, 72

Atomic bomb, 34 ff. *passim,* 41, 46, 47

Authority, 131 ff., 197. *See* Infallibility

Babbitt, Irving, 51

Baptism, 137, 145, 152, 153, 189; immersion, 145, 185, 197; infant, 190 n.

Baptists, 109, 153, 185, 186, 203; Southern, 128, 157

Bible, the: and "churches," 150; function of, 138 ff.; as product of the church, 188; unscriptural use of, 130-47

Biblical stereotypes, 108 f., 136 f., 141 ff., 144

"Bridge" church concept, 171 ff.

Brooks, Phillips, 188

Buddhism, 39

Butler, Justice, 67

Calvin, Calvinism, 135-36, 137

Capitalism, 212

"Catholic," 102

Champaign case, 22 ff., 26-27

Chillingworth, Roger, 130

Christ as sole authority, 99 ff., 113, 131-35 *passim,* 137 ff., 143, 146-47, 149 ff. *passim,* 176-91, 193 ff., 214

Christian Century, v, vi

Christianity: as community, 135 n., 195 f.; essence of, 92; as creator of world community, 40 ff.; its concept of sin, 42 ff.; interpretations of, 179 f.; and science, 41 ff.; social responsibility of, 46

Church, ecumenical, 96 f. *passim,* 98, 219; basis of, 177 f., 186 f.; constitution vs. fellowship in, 181 ff., 188-89, 193; definition of, 149 f.; diversity in, 167 f., 178, 186, 192-96; functions of, 151, 152 ff., 156, 197 f.; and individual, 208; polity of, 204 ff.; results of lack of, 102-3; sacramental character of, 197 f.; theology of, 193 ff.; ways of creating, 154-67, 179 ff.

"Churches" and the church, 97-101 *passim,* 158, 180 ff. *et passim*

Clericalism, 77

Collectivist mind of America, 78 f., 82, 83, 114, 116 *et passim*

Comity, 127, 156

Commercialized entertainment, 16, 49-59; appeal of, 49 f.; effect on mind, 51 ff., 54-55; moral effects of, 50 f.; and religion, 53-54; and technique, 55 ff.

221

Date Due